THE
FRIENDSHIP
CRISIS

THE FRIENDSHIP CRISIS

FINDING, MAKING,
AND KEEPING
FRIENDS
WHEN YOU'RE
NOT A KID ANYMORE

MARLA PAUL

RODALE

© 2004 by Marla Paul

Printed in the United States of America
Rodale Inc. makes every effort to use acid-free ∞, recycled paper ♻.
Book design by Texas Type

Library of Congress Cataloging-in-Publication Data

Paul, Marla.
    The friendship crisis : finding, making, and keeping friends when
you're not a kid anymore / Marla Paul.
       p.   cm.
    ISBN 1–57954–745–1 hardcover
    1. Female friendship.   2. Women—Social networks.   I. Title.
HQ1206.P375 2004
302.3′4′082—dc22   2003022571

Distributed to the book trade by St. Martin's Press

2 4 6 8 10 9 7 5 3 1   hardcover

Visit us on the Web at www.rodalestore.com, or call us toll-free at (800) 848-4735.

WE **INSPIRE** AND **ENABLE** PEOPLE TO IMPROVE
THEIR LIVES AND THE WORLD AROUND THEM

To Paul and Elizabeth

Acknowledgments

I HAVE always been drawn to Native American storyteller dolls, perhaps because I am a gatherer and teller of stories. This book would not have been possible without the generosity of all the women who shared their stories with me. Many thanks to everyone who spoke to, wrote, and e-mailed me.

My husband, Paul, has been a deep well of support while I wrote this book. He read every page to offer his valuable feedback. When I was deciding whether, in fact, to write a book, my daughter, Elizabeth, inspired me by saying if I did, I'd be setting a good example for her. I hope so. She's a great example for me, too, in more ways than she knows.

My agent, Leslie Breed, has been a partner and greatly appreciated cheerleader throughout this whole process, which can be lonely at times. Thanks to Stephanie Tade at Rodale for her passion for this book. My skilled and enthusiastic editor, Jennifer Kushnier, helped hone these pages. She is a writer's dream.

Judy Jordan was always willing to carve out time to share her wisdom about women's friendships and offer encouragement. Her insights have been so important over the years. Linda Hartling was tremendously helpful in locating experts and research. Judi Geake shared her experience in working with hundreds of women's groups. Harriet Mosatche generously assisted my research. Jim Coates kindly and patiently rescued me from every computer fix.

ACKNOWLEDGMENTS

I'd also like to thank Donette Jensen at the Winnetka-Northfield library for her unflagging and unfailingly cheerful efforts to help me track down obscure books and her willingness to renew them, probably more times than she should have. I appreciate the assistance of Tom Smith, who directs the General Social Survey at the University of Chicago's National Opinion Research Center.

Thanks to the past and present editors of the WomanNews section of the *Chicago Tribune*—Jean Rudolph Scott, Wendy Navratil, and Cassandra West—for supporting my column on women's friendship. Bonnie Miller-Rubin offered sharp feedback on a tricky chapter.

I am so grateful to my close friends. My life is much richer because of all of you. My parents, Jan and Al Paul, have always been great supporters as has been my sister, Lisa Paul.

And a special thanks to Rubin Naiman, Jean-Pierre Marques, Karma Kientzler, and Mel Zuckerman.

Contents

PART TWO: THE TANGO OF FRIENDSHIP

PART ONE

The Thieves of Friendship

1

The Hunger for Friends

Why Everybody Feels a Pang

MAYBE there are some women who have never felt lonely for friends, but I doubt it. I believe virtually every woman has moments, or months, or years when she feels her dance card is empty, or at least not completely filled. No one is immune, not even the person who has spent her whole life in the same town and still hangs out with her old high school gang.

Losing companions may happen abruptly. Women yank up roots to relocate for a new job or to trail a spouse. The recently divorced may slip into social isolation.

But often the loss tiptoes up, the unexpected fallout of a hurried life. You race home from the office to ferry your kids to soccer practice and piano, sling dinner on their plates, and wedge in a hurried chat with your husband before you nod off in front of your favorite TV show. Who has time for friends? They're barely a blip on your screen, until your mother is diagnosed with Alzheimer's and suddenly there's no one to call.

Or perhaps now that you've quit your job, you feel like a stranger in your own town. You're pushing your toddler on the swings when you realize you don't know a single mother at the park—though they all seem to know each other. You never really got to know anyone in the neighborhood because your close pals were all at work. "I felt like I had two heads," lamented one of my neighbors when no one talked to her at the playground.

Sometimes you don't even realize what's missing. The only symptom of a friend shortage may be low-level doldrums, a shadowy malaise that you can't quite identify. The full measure of my own isolation smacked me in the head like a beanball when I filled out an emergency card for my daughter's school after I moved to a Chicago suburb. There were spaces for three neighborhood contacts. I didn't have a single name to write in.

Unlike many of our mothers, who sank roots into neighborhoods like ancient oaks—raising children, playing bridge, and drinking coffee with the same women for decades—our paths in the 21st century no longer follow neat parallel tracks. Our lives shift, veer off onto new paths, and old companions fall away. We have babies at wildly different ages or not at all. Our work lives often ricochet from a communal office to a home-based business and back again. We dip in and out of retirement.

Virtually every new life chapter has the potential to disrupt friendships: moving; leaving an office to stay home; divorce; the death of a spouse; retirement; illness. These seismic shifts can topple the walls of community.

But it's not necessarily a cataclysmic event that frays connections. Life chips away at your circle. You may thrive for years in a tight group of buddies, then several take jobs out of state. Interests change. If all your friends are having babies and you're not, you may no longer have much in common with them, or feel they don't have time for you. Shy women may have always been short on companions; for them the frustration is not losing friends, but pushing past their reserve to make them.

Whatever the reason pals are scarce, the impact is the same. It's like missing an essential nutrient. Without friends, problems weigh more and pleasures yield less joy. It's a palpable void.

Nobody expects to come up empty of friends. Men, yes; friends, no. When I was young, I used to creep out of bed and spy on my mother's weekly bridge game, hoots of laughter and gossipy whispers floating up the stairs like a promise. I thought I was witnessing a glimpse of my future. Instead it was the ghost of a fleeting past.

A Cold Bath instead of a Warm Welcome

The problem is not just that friends ineluctably disappear from our lives, but that making new ones is so arduous. We search in a climate that often seems icy and inhospitable. Our skills are as rusty as the old can opener in the back of the drawer. Making friends as children and teens was as effortless as breathing. As midlife women, though, it's suddenly a complicated dance whose steps we try to retrace but can't quite remember.

I resettled in Chicago with my husband and young daughter in 1993, following a five-year stint in Dallas. Every afternoon at dismissal time, I stared enviously at knots of moms clustered around each other's minivans, chatting outside the grammar school door. Once or twice I mustered my courage and plunged into their circle. But I sensed only politeness, not the easy welcome granted to others. After that, I brought magazines to read in the car and pretended it didn't hurt.

Trying to hatch new relationships, I invited women out to lunch, enrolled in a yoga class, became a classroom mom, but my efforts were mostly one-way. When my daughter's first new friend came over to play, I was prepared to warmly greet her mother. I never got the chance. "Hi, when should I pick her up?" she asked breathlessly before zooming off. When another woman dropped off her child, she suggested we meet at the park sometime. But whenever I called she was unavailable.

What was the secret code these other women seemed to instinctively know, and why couldn't I crack it? Was it my faded jeans? Did I laugh too loud? Did I seem too needy?

To prop up my sagging self-confidence and reassure myself that I wasn't a total loser, at school functions I silently recited the mantra, "I'm okay, I'm okay." Corny, but it helped a bit.

The nadir was our grammar school's holiday sing. In the bright, overheated auditorium, women in Christmas sweaters shouted hello and greeted each other like long-lost sisters. Groups clustered up and down the aisles. The cheerful din buzzed in my ears as I perched solo on a metal folding chair.

"We moved to the wrong town!" I wailed to my husband later that night and many others. I was sure the perfect friends, and acceptance, were several miles away in a university community. I was so busy feeling sorry for myself that I failed to notice I wasn't the only woman not partaking in the gabfest.

This was unfamiliar territory for me. Before relocating, I'd always had ready-made companions in an office. But now I worked at home and didn't see a soul all day save the UPS man. While a few close buddies from my earlier days in Chicago were still around, they were ensconced in downtown offices during the week and didn't live nearby. Any get-togethers had to be inscribed in black leather planners (theirs, not mine) weeks or even months in advance. I yearned for women to meet for coffee so we could lament the dearth of Saturday night baby-sitters and the volatility of young girls' friendships.

Because writers have this strange habit of exposing their

foibles, I wrote about my wallflower status in an essay in the *Chicago Tribune*. While I wanted to shine some light on my conundrum, I was mortified when the piece appeared. It's perfectly acceptable to be on the prowl for a man or a partner, but don't go announcing to the world that you're looking for a friend. Women fear we have some glaring personal flaw if we're not flanked by companions. It's like being the only person who doesn't hold an invitation to the party. Surely no one else was in this pickle.

Boy, was I wrong. The essay appeared on a Sunday. By Monday morning my phone was ringing, and by Tuesday the letters began to arrive. People had tracked down my home address and phone number. One woman pulled me aside at a wedding; another grabbed me in the hallway of my daughter's grammar school. Their response and relief were universal: "Thank God, it's not just me!" they said. When I wrote a similar story for *Ladies' Home Journal*, I was also flooded with letters — this time from around the country.

I'd yanked the curtain off a shameful secret, only there is nothing shameful about it. A lot of women are lonely. And it's damn hard to make new friends in our culture of busyness. As we frantically juggle a constellation of demands many of us are unwilling, or unable, to fold a new pal into our lives.

How hard is it? When a Chicago-area therapist recognized the isolation of her female clients, she launched a service that fixed women up with friends instead of romantic partners. After she placed an ad in the newspaper, she was swamped by people wanting to sign up — some of whom, amazingly, lived in the same high-rise building or on the same block. One of the reasons it's so difficult to find new companions, she surmised, is because nobody realizes other people are looking, too. "If you're not wearing a sign, nobody knows," she says.

In another sign of friendship hunger, several alternative newspapers now run ads in a "friends wanted" section, a move sparked by reader demand. And at a popular New York singles club called Social Circles, 90 percent of the people who join say it's to make friends, a hike from 60 percent five years ago.

Loneliness Is Not Your Destiny

Much has already been written about the glories of women's friendships. Yet a lot of us feel like we're standing outside in the rain, hungrily peering in through the window at the buffet. The truth is, that party might not be as big as you think. In fact, the idealized fantasy we weave about other people's companionship may be just that.

So I began writing a column on women's friendship for the *Tribune* to explore this dilemma and chronicle women's efforts to find new companions. Over the years, hundreds of women have generously shared their stories with me. I listened to their frustration, anger, and hurt. But as we kept in touch, I also cheered their successes because they eventually forged rich, new relationships. I did, too. These pages tell what we've learned.

It turns out bouts of loneliness are universal but not incurable. Friends are a renewable resource, thank heavens. It may not feel that way when you're perched by yourself in the bleachers at your daughter's soccer game or sitting home on a Saturday night when your married friends are going out to dinner. But even the most isolated women I interviewed ultimately found satisfying companionship. It took perseverance and creative strategies, but it did happen. This book offers their blueprint for success. Loneliness is not a life sentence, just a natural, temporary interlude.

2

Friendship Bandits

WHEN my cousin's family tossed her a surprise 40th birthday party, only her closest girlfriends were invited. As a swarm of women clustered in the darkened living room waiting for my unsuspecting cousin, I was shocked at the depth of my envy. The invitation list for any party of mine would be sparse. Throughout the night, a constellation of adoring pals swirled around her, nibbling smoked salmon canapés as they hooted over past adventures and plotted future trips to antique stores and flea markets. "I'll call you!" they promised each other. My own calendar had never seemed emptier.

As I drove home from the celebration in the chilly night, I brooded over how I could have reached 44 and not have enough friends. Weren't they supposed to have accrued over the years? What had gone wrong? Logically, of course, I knew. My circle of pals had fractured when I moved back to Chicago from Dallas, and working at home had quashed the chance of meeting new people in an office. But understanding was small consolation.

We are raised believing friendship is a birthright of our sex. Most of us still remember the names of our mothers' closest friends when we were kids because these women were such fixtures in their lives. We glimpse the snug orbit of women and their pals on TV shows and in movies. An avalanche of recent books trumpets the pleasures of female friends. When we don't have them, or they're in short supply, we feel we've failed in an essential life skill or that the universe has egregiously short-changed us.

The numerous women I've interviewed and heard from in letters and e-mails reveal that social ties are frayed in many lives. Our precarious lives are raided by friendship thieves. For many women in midlife, the biggest felon is the squeeze of time. We can barely stretch a day to contain a job, our kids, our spouse, and maybe a 2-mile run, let alone a relaxing dinner with a buddy at the new tapas restaurant in town. So we cancel the dinner date with her for the second time in 2 months, perhaps cracking a tiny fissure in the relationship, one that could widen if we don't pay attention.

Moving, children, divorce, leaving work, widowhood, and retirement also shear us from companions. We brace for the loss when we're geographically separated from friends. But it's a rude slap when the cause is simply life twisting in a new direction. Can't a divorced woman stay close to her married buddies? Can't a single woman retain her pals who have children? Yes, but it's a challenge. We want companions who understand our experiences, who know what it's like to sit up five bleary nights in a row with a feverish kid or face a blind date—palms damp, stomach cartwheeling—for the first time in 20 years. The women who preserve their shifting friendships work hard at it.

It's an ongoing struggle because life skitters like a leaf in the wind. If you're divorced this year and find single friends, they may drift off if you or they remarry. Three of my friends just announced that they are moving to far-flung vacation houses in other states once they retire; I'll be lucky to see them a few times a year.

Those whose pals slip away are left flailing in a society with fewer life rafts. More of us are living without a partner as the number of the never-married and divorced climbs. Many people also live far from their families, which is another loss of support. And social surveys show we've become increasingly alienated from our community, as membership plunges in women's civic organizations, religious groups, and clubs.

On soft summer nights, instead of loitering on our lawns and grousing to neighbors about the mosquitoes, we're sealed in our air-conditioned houses staring at the computer monitor or a giant TV screen, its icy-blue glow illuminating the window like a postmodern Edward Hopper painting. As we spend less time with our neighbors, we're cheated of effortless socializing, the kind that doesn't require jumping in the car or pulling out a day planner. One woman, who juggles a demanding career and care of her two daughters, yearns for women to hang out with on her block. "We could see each other in the evening and have the casual conversations that don't require a lot of planning," she says wistfully, recalling the chats she witnessed between her mother and neighbors in New York City.

In a vestige of a friendlier, more connected past, the older couples in my neighborhood, who have lived in their modest ranch homes for 40 years, pull up webbed lawn chairs on each other's driveways after dinner. They talk quietly as the last evening light ebbs and clusters of fireflies flash their private code of chartreuse lights. When the couples finally fold up their chairs, the crickets are trilling. The people who moved here more recently are invisible on these evenings save for a few dog walkers. I rock on my front porch swing after dinner, hoping to trip a few neighbors. But all I see of them are their minivans disappearing into the yawn of electric garage doors. We wave.

The Symptoms of a Friend Shortage

Regardless of why we're short on pals at a particular time, the emotional fallout is the same. And it feels lousy. Not surprisingly, research has shown that loneliness affects our personality, making us more anxious, angry, pessimistic, and stressed.

"Loneliness is visceral," says Leslie Levine, the author of *Will This Place Ever Feel Like Home?*, who moved from Rochester, New York, to a Chicago suburb. "I can feel it in my bones. It's an empty, hollow, faraway feeling, like my feet aren't on the ground. You don't feel tethered, you don't have your anchors."

Sandy, a 51-year-old social worker with two young sons, describes herself as withering after she relocated to a new state. "It was as if I was a plant that had been yanked out of the soil and transplanted someplace where I couldn't thrive."

Isolation painted my life sepia and trailed me like a shadow. After feeling rebuffed in my efforts to forge new friendships, my heart snapped shut. When I bumped into a woman I knew slightly at a plant sale, she said pleasantly, "It's nice to see you." "Liar!" I thought to myself. And when someone said she'd missed me after I'd been absent for a few months from my book club, I was stunned. I didn't think anyone noticed whether I showed up.

A lot of women have these experiences in our frenetically mobile society. The cousin that roused my jealousy has, thus far, led the rare stable existence. She's lived with her family in the same suburb for 20 years, just a few miles from her childhood home. She's retained her high school friends, sorority sisters from a state university, and folded in a layer of her neighbors for a rich parfait of pals. But most of us aren't this fortunate. Our college friends may live in distant states. Our neighborhoods may change every five years. Our hometowns may be places we visit only once a year. We've got to work harder to have friends.

But we absolutely can have them. Yes, there are stages in our lives—from moving to quitting a job to getting divorced—that may threaten and even topple our friendships. But with awareness of the flashing red danger zones, sometimes we can prevent the loss. If not, we can find new friends. Numerous women have rebuilt their circles from the ground up with hard work, a bit of plotting, and a large dose of patience. You can, too.

3

Too Busy for Friends

Not Enough Hours in the Day

BEFORE Sharon sinks into an exhausted sleep at night, she sometimes tallies the number of people who would attend her funeral. She doesn't suffer from any health problems that inspire her dark bedtime fantasy. She's just bereft about the lack of intimates that would bid her farewell. "I think, what I if I died right now? There would be three people at my funeral: my husband and my kids. Isn't that sad?"

Most of us don't worry about our "final guest list," but Sharon's lament about her barren social life is echoed by many women who work outside the home. Employed, married women with children are the most free-time-deprived people in the country. A February 2002 *Child* magazine survey found that before having children, women spend 14 hours per week with friends, but they spend only five hours after having kids. "Visits with friends are now on the social capital endangered species list," writes Robert D. Putnam in his book *Bowling Alone.*

Indeed, many women shove friendship to the stone-cold back burner. As Sharon, 44, a newspaper columnist in Seattle, explains, "I am truly overwhelmed. There are so many things pressing on me just to meet the basics, just to go to bed at night and feel like an adequate mother—not even good, just adequate. I have a hierarchy of human imperatives: the first is financial survival, the next is being a decent parent. There aren't any hours in the day after that."

But Sharon realizes her hierarchy exacts a steep price. She mournfully recalls a potential friendship that slipped away because she was too busy. "The most wonderful woman reached out to me in the kindest way. I loved this woman right away. She'd call me up in one of the endless rains and say, 'How are you doing?' She invited me to join a support group with four other women; she invited us over to her house. I didn't feel I had the time, even though I needed it. It was a lost opportunity. I was so busy getting things done—sign your kids up for this, meet this deadline, go for that raise—that I wasn't thinking of the subtler but more profound joys of life, like friendship."

Unfortunately, Sharon is not alone in her unwillingness to embrace a new friend. Yankelovich Partners report that in 2001, 32 percent of women surveyed said they have "very little room in my life for new friends."

Most women, like Brenda, 44, a communications specialist in Milwaukee, crave more girlfriends but can't figure out when to make them. "I keep planning to have a night out with some women I've just met, but I never do it. I get home from the office and I'm tired. I just want to go to sleep," she admits with a sigh. "On the weekends, I am loath to take away any time with my kids." She, too, feels cheated by the shortage of companions. "There is a really huge loss when you don't have enough friends. It's not supposed to be like that. Friendship is one of life's delights. As much as you love your spouse and your family, you need friends, too. I agonize over what to do about it."

Some women cope by pruning second-string pals. "There are friends I've chosen not to see because I can't fit any more in," confesses Amy, 45, who has two young children and works part time in Denver. "There are friends I see twice a year, if I'm lucky, because my life is so full." She tries for a weekly call to her best friend, a single woman, but only manages to see her once a month. "We have these conversations where she says, 'Have I done something wrong?' [because we haven't spoken in a while]. I say, 'No, no, no. It's nothing you've done!'" Amy can't imagine finding space in her life for new people. "It's as if you've reached the fill mark on the gauge." But Amy was on the flip side of that sad equation when she briefly lived in Washington, D.C. "I had women tell me they thought I was really nice but they didn't have time for any more friends. It really broke my heart."

It doesn't have to be like this.

⊶✦⊷

SOLUTIONS

Women Who Find the Time

What separates busy women who have time for friends from those who don't? Attitude. These women value themselves enough to put their girlfriends ahead of their family and work a few times a week. They know their offspring and mates will not suffer irreparable damage if they toss them the phone number of the local pizza place before waltzing out the door for a weekly yoga class with a pal. (Hell, let 'em look up the pizza phone number themselves.) While these women also have limited time to devote to pals, they spackle them into the cracks of their lives. They realize friends are essential to a solid foundation, a necessity, not a luxury. Here's how and why they do it.

HOLLY: CLEAR PRIORITIES

It's hard to imagine a more hourly challenged woman than Holly, 51, an executive for a national nonprofit company in New York City. After a full day in the office, she often races to a night meeting, speaks to parent groups, consults with private clients, or hunkers down to write one of her string of books. She

---

No Excuses Strategy List

A jammed schedule is no reason to ditch your pals. Just try these multitasking ways to keep up and keep in touch.

1. Work out together—meet at the gym or hoof it on the walking path.
2. Meet for early morning coffee or breakfast before work.
3. Take a class together. It guarantees you'll meet once a week.
4. Swoop in for quick, impromptu visits when you're in the neighborhood. (It doesn't hurt to call a few minutes ahead.)
5. Walk your dogs together. Or tag along while she walks her dog.
6. Invite her over for dessert after dinner. Or meet for an ice-cream cone.
7. Strap on a headset so you can chat while you sort laundry or rinse the romaine.
8. If she's committed to her kid's twice weekly soccer game, hang out in the stands together. Or tool along on an errand. One woman accompanied her friend on nighttime car rides to lull her new baby to sleep.
9. Schedule your manicures, pedicures, or highlights together.
10. Scoop out the hamper and hit the Laundromat or your apartment building's laundry room. Washing your clothes isn't nearly as tedious as a duo.
11. If you can't physically be together, watch your favorite TV show, say *Sex in the City* or *Friends*, while you're on the phone together. It's almost like sitting in her den.

---

also has a husband, a teenage son and daughter, and an ailing mother-in-law, whom she visits on weekends. It would seem that a seven-day week could barely contain all her responsibilities, let alone dates with girlfriends. Yet, it does. And not only for longtime pals, but for new ones who appear. "Friendships are a very important part of my life. I make the time for them," says Holly, a warm woman with a quick laugh, who credits her buddies as her stress relievers.

How does Holly fit them in? By including them in her gym workouts and fitness walks during lunch and on weekends. One Saturday morning at the health club, Holly vented about a work crisis to her friend, Debbie, as they pedaled on the bikes. Hopping on the stair-step machines, Debbie, whose mother had died a few months earlier, described how awful it was to clean out the apartment. "If we hadn't gone to the gym it would have been difficult to fit that in, " Holly says.

Holly recently met Rachel, with whom she felt an instant rapport. The challenge was capturing a mote of space in her life for a new person. The solution—frequent e-mails and dinner every couple months—wasn't ideal for Rachel, who desired more contact, but she accepted Holly's limitations. "She knows I'm much busier than she is," says Holly. They always schedule their next date before they pay the check. E-mails keep them linked to the daily events in each other's lives, which is essential, Holly believes, for a satisfying relationship.

BETH: APPLYING THE GLUE

Beth's house is a mess, and dinner isn't looking too good, either. It'll be either macaroni out of a box—if there's any in the pantry—or carryout pizza, if there isn't. "My floor will suck up the soles of your shoes," Beth cheerfully acknowledges, but she doesn't apologize for any domestic shortcomings. After a grinding day as a graphic designer, freelancing at night, and tending to her husband and teenage daughter, she has only one "hobby." "I nurture relationships," says Beth, 51, who lives outside Phoenix. "I can only do a couple things well. This is one of the things I've chosen. The quality of your relationships is everything. It gives a sense of richness to my life."

At 9 P.M. Beth sweeps everything else aside to catch up with friends by phone. She calls it the glue of her relationships and applies it generously. But face time is vital, too. After work, Beth often cruises by her neighbor, Cheryl's, house for a microburst of conversation or gossip, usually on the excuse of an errand. Likewise, Cheryl often rings Beth's bell with a sample of her latest home-baked treat—say, a slice of still-warm pineapple cake. And whenever Beth works in her company's downtown office instead of her suburban-based branch, she always schedules lunch with a colleague. "Sometimes I'd just like to shop, but I try to see people to cultivate and strengthen those bonds," she says.

"If somebody said about me, 'She kept every friend she ever made,' it would be like giving me the Oscar and the Tony all rolled into one," muses Beth.

LIZ: THE MASTER MULTITASKER

"You can't squeeze any more hours in the day, so you have to make use of the hours you have," says Liz, 43, who has three kids and runs her own career counseling firm in Boston. Enter her cell phone and headset. If she's not making business calls on the drive to her downtown office, she phones friends. At home, she straps on her headset and gabs with pals while she makes beds, folds laundry, and cooks dinner. "Occasionally, you have to put a friend on hold and say, 'I'm running the water now,'" Liz says with a laugh. She uses any five-minute window to stay connected. "I don't have the 'let's sit down and have a cup of coffee and talk' kind of hours. I don't do a lot of traditional things well, like lunches. Given my schedule, if I was relying on that I would have lost touch with a lot of people." She calls herself the ultimate multitasker, even meeting up with neighbors and friends while she walks her new standard poodle.

Busy women need forgiving friends who don't stand on ceremony or stew over unreturned phone calls, says Liz. "Sometimes I call them back or they call me back, figuring I didn't pick up the message or my kids didn't give it to me" (good assumption). One friend, who finally captured her—not the machine—on the phone, greeted her with the friendly jibe, "What, did you fall off the face of the earth?" "There is this mutual understanding," Liz notes, "that we want to be friends, but it's a really busy world and everybody is trying to keep a lot of balls in the air."

Even with all the balls spinning, Liz still makes new pals. "I would hate to close myself off to new friends. New friends mean new ideas, new interests, new activities." So when an engaging woman drops into her orbit, Liz seizes the opportunity to get to know her. "If I had to see the same people every day I'd be tapping my foot," she says.

KAREN: WHO NEEDS SLEEP?

It would be easy for Karen, 31, to plead no time for friends. On an easy week she logs 50 hours at her job as a financial manager of mergers and acquisitions for a pharmaceutical company on the East Coast. During high throttle, she's stuck in the office for 70 hours a week plus two hours daily commuting time. But in spite of her often brutal hours, several nights a week she's out for sushi or clubbing with companions. "What keeps me sane, what keeps my job in perspective, are the friends in my life. They make me happy," says Karen, a single woman with a boyfriend. If something has to give, and sometimes it does, it's a few hours of sleep. She schedules her social life with the same attentiveness and planning she uses for work—e-mailing a woman in June, for example, to set up a night out for her birthday in July.

Taking Your Social Pulse

Still, life can swamp us even when we have the best intentions. Chris Essex, codirector of the Center for Work and Family in Rockville, Maryland, makes her living counseling people on how to find balance in their lives. Her prescription includes a big dose of time with pals. But she lost her own equilibrium, tumbling into isolation, when her father became ill with Alzheimer's. Overwhelmed by frequent plane trips to see him, a hectic work schedule, and family demands, she neglected her social life. The fallout: Essex was depleted. Her husband couldn't give her all the support she needed in dealing with her parents, and she wasn't seeing friends to take up the slack. Her zest was flickering for lack of oxygen.

That's when she pressed her finger to her emotional pulse and realized the healer needed her own medicine. "I think I need to have more fun," she mused to a pal. So Essex issued a clarion call to friends to have lunch, browse antique stores, shop for clothes. "I realized I had to take better care of myself to compensate for the drain from my parents," she says. Essex boosted time with pals to the top of her priority list and pushed errands to the bottom. "I'm laughing more now," she adds.

But Essex says she and other women are never cured of toppling off the tightrope. As work travel ratchets up and her free time compresses, she recognizes that "this is an ongoing maintenance issue. You don't get to say, 'I'm done, I graduate.' It's a process that needs to be attended to. I'm bound and determined to attend to it because it's a really important piece in my life."

When you decide to take time for your buddies, they'll fit into your life like the long-missing pieces of a puzzle. Once they snap into place, the picture is complete. Everything else—work and connections with your spouse, kids, or romantic partner—will magically seem better. It's called taking care of yourself.

4

Pint-Sized Wrecking Balls

Can Friendships Survive Kids?

ONE after another, Cathy lists the once-close pals she no longer sees, including two former best friends. The friendships' cause of death: marriage and children. "When a friend gets pregnant, she'll say our relationship is not going to change," says Cathy, 46, who is divorced and childless. She knows better.

When a friend becomes a mother, a childless woman immediately senses tremors under her feet. The single friend now has to cope with her old pal's unavailability, utter preoccupation with her progeny, and exquisite sensitivity to any suggestion that these children may not be the most fascinating creatures ever to grace the earth. The friend is expected to twist happily into a pretzel to fit the new shape of the mother's life. On the flip side, the harried new mom must parry her clueless friend's demands to meet for a happy hour cocktail and hang out like old times. She's annoyed that her pal doesn't grasp the hurricane that is now her life. Their colliding needs are a potential recipe for a small nuclear explosion. The fallout may be a permanent winter for the relationship.

Cathy, who sells medical supplies, revisits and analyzes her losses, wondering, "Is it me? Am I being selfish?" Of this much she is sure: the most solid foundation can irreparably crack when babies come along. Her best friend, Fran, disappeared after one apparently fatal transgression: Cathy stopped going to her kids' birthday parties. For several years, Cathy had gallantly cohosted the fetes, dishing out pizza and leading scavenger hunts like the Pied Piper. But then she'd had enough. When Fran invited her to the next few gatherings, Cathy concocted lame excuses, not knowing how to explain the truth. "I thought if I was honest, it would be the demise of the friendship." After the declined invitations, Fran's calls to her tapered off and she turned cool. "I thought, 'Fine, two can play this game,'" says Cathy, who also pulled back. "It was childish," she admits. But even if she had discussed her feelings with Fran, she doesn't think the outcome would have changed. A few years later, Fran saw Cathy in the doctor's office and ignored her.

Cathy's friendship with her other best pal, Ruth, blew up on an ill-fated visit to Ruth's new house in North Carolina. "I hadn't seen her in three years," recalls Cathy. "I was anticipating a really fun time. It was a disaster." During the five-day trip, Ruth never hired a sitter for her 3-year-old son. "We never even left the house. I hadn't seen the sights. We couldn't even have a girls' night out," Cathy says, still exasperated. When she gently asked if they could do something by themselves for a day, Ruth "got ticked off." Once back home in Pennsylvania, Cathy sent flowers and a card thanking Ruth for the stay. She left messages for her friend at work and at home. Ruth never called back. "We were best friends for seven years. One comment and that was it. It still bothers me," Cathy says.

Tips for Moms

1. Leave the baby or the kids with your partner, a grandmother, or a sitter once in a while so you can have kid-free time together.

2. Keep the conversation balanced. It's fine to gush over your daughter's brilliant play at the soccer match or fret over your son's friendship woes, but don't blather endlessly about your children.

3. Make sure you ask about your friend's life and listen well. You may not relate personally to her career travails or boyfriend blues, but you can still be interested in her feelings about them.

4. Acknowledge that your friend's schedule is important, too. If she's always making the drive to see you, head out to her turf on occasion if possible.

5. Crack out of the usual mold and try something different together— say, an edgy new play, a kayaking lesson, or volunteering at an animal shelter. Sharing new adventures keeps the friendship fresh.

The strain of dueling lifestyles has unraveled other relationships for Cathy. She loathes outings with women and their kids because the friend spends the time shouting, "Don't do that!" Ditto perching on a park bench watching you-know-who. "You don't have a conversation. It's, 'Look, he's on the swings! Look, she can go down the slide by herself!'" she groans.

Cathy's met some new friends— ironically, she says, in singles bars. "You go out trying to meet men and you come home with women's phone numbers," she says wryly. But she hasn't been able to find the depth of companionship she lost, women with whom she could have candid and searching conversations.

Pat, a 46-year-old massage therapist in Salt Lake City, also struggles with married pals. She was in the shower when she heard the phone machine click on one Sunday. "Hi, we're at the Kiddie Fair, and Jordan is on the pony ride. Why don't you come over and meet us?" Still dripping, Pat punched the erase button. An hour later, the phone jangled again, the same persistent friend nudging, "Come and meet us if you're home." Pat burst into tears. "They mean well, but they don't get it," she says of this friend and every other who tries to fold her into their families. "I don't have a kid and I don't have a husband. They feel like they can substitute what they have for what I don't have—'Here's your makeshift family.' It makes me feel sad." Nearly all of her longtime friends are now married with children. Their once-easy relationships have shifted, stirring up more angst than pleasure when she sees them.

It's awkward for her to tag along with married friends. "I think their husbands are saying, 'Oh, here she comes again.' I feel like a fifth wheel," she explains. Hanging out with her friends' kids also smarts because it reminds her of what she doesn't have. "I've always wanted children. To be around them all the time kills me."

Tips for Non-Moms

1. It's hard to truly grasp the seismic changes a baby wreaks unless you've got one. But you can try. Don't take your friend's preoccupation with that squalling creature personally. This is a period when you'll need to give more than you get.

2. Be patient. An equilibrium of sorts will eventually return to the relationship.

3. Stay connected with her by offering to help. Bring over dinner, then hold the baby so she can eat a rare meal in peace.

4. Don't turn it into a power struggle. Realize you may have to make more compromises to see her.

5. Suggest you, she, and the kids head to the zoo, the beach, or even a movie once in a while. It's important to the friendship that you connect with her children.

What Pat needs are women who can spontaneously grab a burger with her after work. "I have to find someone who has the same lifestyle," she says. So Pat flits to new friends, but those nascent relationships feel thinner, less satisfying. "I don't open up as much with the next one and the next one. I'm not real secure with them," she admits. The only two women she can count on are her two sisters. "Thank God for them," she says.

The Deep Freeze: A Mom's Perspective

Why do new moms jettison single friends like so much ballast? It's because a childless friend can't understand the new contours of the relationship and accept the radical shift in a new mom's priorities. That's why Ann was ready to dump Dana, although she'd been a trusted friend for nearly a decade. After Ann's daughter was born, Dana was oblivious to the change in her pal's life. "She couldn't understand why I couldn't spend all day Saturday shopping with the baby," recalls Ann, 28, a former analyst for the Central Intelligence Agency in Washington, D.C. That wasn't the only problem. Dana was also sensitivity-impaired. When the baby began taking her first wobbly steps — a thrilling time for a mom — Dana would jab, "She's not very good at that, is she?" "It might have seemed innocuous to her, but it cut me to the core," Ann fumes. And when the toddler began to babble, Dana admonished, "Not now, dear! Mommy and I are talking." Or, Dana babbled back in a way that seemed like she was poking fun.

"Dana couldn't handle the competition," explains Ann. So she stopped phoning her and ignored Dana's messages. "I did the same thing I'd do with men I wanted to leave me alone. But she didn't get the hint. She kept calling." Unsure of what to do, Ann asked other women for advice online. She heard from one who had been painfully ditched, without explanation, by a friend. Tell her the truth, the woman advised. So the next time Dana called, Ann did exactly that. "I said she seemed unable to understand that my life and priorities had changed. I couldn't do things on the weekend because it was the only time we could be together as a family. And when we did do things, I wasn't going to put her with a baby-sitter." A tearful Dana said she'd do whatever was necessary to stay pals. The next Friday, she took off work so the three of them could go to the zoo. The friendship soon regained its former warmth. Dana was the first person Ann called when she got back from a vacation.

Dana and Ann reconciled because Dana was willing to compromise and accept significantly new terms for the relationship. She received less than she wanted, which was for Ann to be the same friend she was before the baby. But that wasn't going to happen. For Dana, it was worth yielding to Ann's needs to retain her friendship.

But some relationships cannot survive a child tossed into the mix. Ann was unable to hold on to her "brunch friends," a married, childless couple she and her husband had met every Sunday. Perhaps she should have seen it coming when she asked them to be her new daughter's guardians and they refused. Once the baby arrived, those brunches became history. "They stopped inviting us," says a flabbergasted Ann. "The few times we've suggested it, they had other things to do. We feel dumped. It hurts my feelings a lot. They were really good friends." Since then, the couple has invited them over "individually" for a movie and dinner, suggesting that Ann and her husband split the evening. The message: no babies wanted here.

When Kids Fight, Moms Do, Too

It's natural for moms to become close when their kids do. They see each other all the time—dropping off and picking up for play dates—and have their children's connection in common. But while it's an easy way to hook up with a pal, it's also a potentially dangerous one. Nearly every woman has a story of how a dustup between her kid and his friend wrecked her friendship with the other mom. If the kids fight or split— as often happens as they bounce around in their friendships—the moms' bond becomes as vulnerable as hyacinths in a hard frost. The women are faced with the delicate task of extricating their relationship from that of their children.

It isn't easy. Normally mild-mannered women unsheathe their claws when someone is mean to their kids. And even if you rationally know that it's not the other mother's fault that her Brandon ditched or punched your Adam, it's hard not to let your emotions spill over to her, too.

These mom friendships are actually highly salvageable, but you must proceed with caution. Moms of warring children need to discuss the situation in a neutral way, never bad-mouthing or blaming another woman's child. That's a good way to kiss the friendship good-bye. Women become wildly defensive at even a whiff of criticism about their unassailable progeny.

That's what Rona, 49, discovered when her friend Betsy's 11-year-old daughter began tormenting Rona's 10-year-old daughter on their play dates. The girl usually played at Rona's Dallas home because Betsy, a single mom, worked full time and Rona didn't. But the girl's once-likeable personality changed. "She became snobby, very materialistic and bossy," says Rona. The girl, who lived in a wealthy community, mocked Rona's daughter's nondesigner clothes. She also decided all the games they played and then insisted Rona's daughter clean up the mess. Rona's daughter started dreading their play dates. Then Rona witnessed this behavior firsthand when the girl didn't know she was watching. In a game of "dogs," the girl screamed at Rona's daughter, "Beg! Beg! Beg!" Rona's daughter, who was on her knees and near tears, put up with it for a few minutes, then leaped up and said, "I refuse to do this." "It was just nasty," Rona recalls with a shudder. So what to do?

Rona called Betsy, whom she considered "a wonderful woman." Her plan was to be diplomatically vague. "I said the kids were not getting along as well as they had in the past and they needed a break from each other," Rona says. But Betsy pressed her for details, so Rona elaborated. "I said, 'Your daughter is being bossy with mine.' She refused to believe what happened. She said, 'Emily is never bossy. You must have misheard. My daughter would never do those kinds of things.' She was questioning my credibility," Rona says.

"I haven't spoken to her in over a year," Rona notes regretfully. "Our kids' friendship screwed up a good adult friendship."

For that reason and others, Daryl, 51, is staying mum about the two best friends of her 12-year-old son, Nicky, who ganged up on him during their four-week stay at summer camp. "They threw rocks at him. They hit him with a tennis racket. He was really, really hurt and upset and wanted to come home," says Daryl, who was plenty upset herself. But she isn't saying a word to the mothers of the boys. "They are very good friends of mine. After he got home I wanted to avoid them because I was mad at their children for being mean to my kid and ruining his summer camp experience. What do you say? 'Your son is a beast?'" Daryl is also angry at the women themselves, admitting it's irrational because they don't even know what happened.

She's decided to let her son resolve the situation himself. "I know he will come to me if he is in over his head and doesn't know what to do," Daryl says. "If I talked to the mothers, the mothers would talk to the kids and they would retaliate. I would be making it worse for Nicky. He'd be seen as a tattletale." She also believes a chat about this would not go well with the women, as much as she likes them. "Your first thought is to defend your children. I don't want to get into a pissing match."

Cynthia was on the flip side of that equation when her 13-year old son, Zack, dumped his longtime best friend, Jesse. Her experience offers a window into the awkward plight of a mother whose kid has hurt your kid, but who can't do anything about it. She didn't know how to broach the subject with Jesse's mom, who was her good friend.

Zack and Jesse had been inseparable since they met in first grade. Jesse had sat at their family dinner table so often that

---

Staying Friends with "Sophie's" Mom

Just because your daughter and her best pal, Sophie, are sparring doesn't mean you have to forfeit your friendship with Sophie's mom. Here's some advice for staying close even when your kids break up.

1. If the kids' rocky relationship is affecting your friendship with the mom, you need to talk about it. Keep the conversation neutral and nonjudgmental. Simply bring the issue out into the open. "Don't overidentify with your child's hurt or carry the battle to an adult level," warns Marti von Kluck, a Chicago-area school social worker who has counseled hundreds of students and parents about friendship issues. "Keep your friendship separate from the kids' friendship."

2. Don't criticize her child or assign blame.

3. Indicate your desire to remain close. You could say, "Kari and Sophie are having so many problems. I hope we can continue to be good friends regardless of what the kids decide. I don't want our relationship to be dependent on their relationship," suggests von Kluck.

4. Realize you will have to invest more energy in the friendship if you no longer have your kids drawing you together. You'll have to pick up the phone to stay in touch and make plans to see each other.

5. Be pleasant to your child's former friend.

Cynthia, a 48-year-old at-home mom in Seattle, considered him her "extra son." In junior high, the boys played in a rock band together, but just before freshman year of high school, Zack quit that band to start a new one. He didn't invite Jesse to join. Around that time, Jesse stopped coming to the house. "Where's Jesse?" Cynthia asked Zack. "What happened?" Zack's terse reply: "Stay out of it, Mom."

"That's when I realized you have no control over whom your children are friends with. My son dumped Jesse," says Cynthia sadly. While she never directly raised the issue with Jesse's mom, she expressed to her how much she missed him. "Well, yeah..." his mom said with a chill in her voice. "I wish we had talked about it," laments Cynthia. "I felt guilty about something I didn't do. I think it would have been nice to have it out in the open. I could have apologized for my son, even though all your kid's actions aren't reflections of you." The women managed to stay friends, but they weren't as close. Their children's riff was a wound between them that never properly healed. But their distance was also because they no longer saw each other every day through their sons' activities. "I used to talk to her every single day. Now I see her every month or so," says Cynthia.

As Cynthia discovered, if you don't air the problem, it becomes the elephant in the room that can squash your friendship. Of course, if all you have in common with the other mom is your kids, once they part there's not much to save between the two of you. But if you had developed a strong, separate bond, then talk. Don't try to fix your kids' problems (unless they're very young), says Harriet Mosatche, a developmental psychologist who pens online advice columns for www.girlscouts.org and is the author of *Too Old for This, Too Young for That!* The purpose of your conversation is to recognize how the issue may affect your relationship.

Mosatche suggests initiating this conversation by saying, "I see our kids aren't spending as much time together. The relationship seems to have changed in some way. Have you noticed that, too?" "Your goal is to keep your friendship open and close," Mosatche says.

There is a spectrum of other children-related issues that can challenge your friendships. Perhaps you and your husband are longtime pals with Sheila and Bruce. When your respective kids were young, you always invited the whole family over and vice versa. But now your kids think their kids are annoying. A chat about this is probably a bad idea. It's easier to shift the friendship to adults-only get-togethers. Nobody is insulted when you say, "Let's go out for an adult dinner. Then we can really relax and talk."

Rona has made a pact with two friends never to include any of their kids when they get together. And in a rare instance where honesty worked, she told one friend with wild young children who smeared brownies on her walls, jumped on her bed, and tormented her pets, "I love you, but I don't love how your kids behave when they come to my house." The women decided to go out sans kids or to the friend's house if she was stranded with her children. "I don't care if *her* house gets destroyed," Rona says. As the kids grew up, they actually became civilized human beings.

Time cures many of these problems. As kids grow older and become more independent, you'll be less involved in their social lives. By high school, the only contact you may have with the parents of your kid's new pal is a phone call to ask if they'll be home to chaperone the party on Saturday night. But until kids reach the age where your social lives fork, their friendships can ruffle yours. Some will ineluctably fall away. But others you can keep by facing the issue head on.

SOLUTIONS

Saving the Friendship

Not all single versus married-with-kids friendships hit the skids. But most that survive and thrive require flexibility, empathy for the other's experience, and commitment to the relationship as a separate entity from a husband and kids.

Jillian and Marcia score high on all these points, which is why the former high school buddies remain terrific friends even though Marcia added a husband, a son, a daughter, a parakeet, and a dog to her life. Marcia wouldn't dream of inviting Jillian, who isn't married, to her kids' plays or birthday parties. "I would never expect her to want to go. I don't think she should be obligated. I wouldn't want to subject her to a bunch of screaming children," she says thoughtfully. She prefers to include Jillian in lower-key family dinners.

In their nearly daily conversations, Marcia will share the diagnosis of her daughter's head-to-toe rash—but is careful not to overdo the kid news. "I think it would be boring for her. I want to know what's going on in Jillian's life and what she's feeling. And there are other things in my life besides children," says Marcia, 44, who works as a paralegal and aerobics instructor. She also carves out separate time to be together, parking the kids with her spouse some Sundays to drive into Minneapolis so the two women can cruise an art fair or cycle at the health club.

On her end, Jillian has honed the art of retaining the married friends she cares about. She accepts the limitations of Laura, who always invites her over to be with the family, but will never make separate time for the two of them. "We had a fight over it. I said, 'You never make time for just me,'" says Jillian, a

43-year-old floral designer. The friend flatly told her that wouldn't happen until the children were older. Jillian felt bruised, but she made peace with it. "Laura is so nonjudgmental. I can share anything with her. I know she would be there for me in a second if I needed her."

Jillian adores her friends' family dinners, holidays, and parties. "I live vicariously through what their kids are doing." Jillian thinks she's so warmly welcomed, in part, because she befriends the husbands of her girlfriends. "They marry me, too," she jokes. What stings, however, is not being invited to the social parties of her couple friends because she doesn't have a mate.

Karen, 31, willingly stretches to accommodate her "mom" friends. "They have more responsibilities than I do. I can sympathize," she says. So she squeezes into the spaces on their calendars and endures rush hour gridlock from the city to the suburbs to meet them for dinner, even after a grueling day at her job as a financial manager for an East Coast pharmaceutical company. "It's just not as fun [as it used to be]," she admits. "We won't be going out dancing till 4 in the morning like I do with my core of friends who are single." Still, these women consider each other as close as family and have vowed to stay together for a lifetime of dinners, birthday parties, and Christmases. When they meet, she's riveted by stories about their kids. "They open a whole new world for me. I want to have kids. I listen so I know, 'So that's how you burp the baby. So your boobs swell up when you don't pump.' They can teach me."

The landscape of the friendship will inevitably shift between single and married friends with kids. Hedgerows sprout in an open field of grass. And it's often hardest on the single friend, who needs to do the most accommodating. Still, with mutual sensitivity, many women can stay pals. Infants eventually grow up and go to school all day, leave for college, and then marry. A friend will still be at your side.

5

"First I Lost My Husband, Then I Lost My Friends"

*How to Jump-Start Your Social Life
after Being Divorced or Widowed*

AFTER Kristin's divorce from her husband of 14 years, she cracked open her black leather address book to set up a dinner date. When she called two married women friends, each one told her to phone back when she was dating someone. As she slowly hung up the phone, a dawning awareness chilled her. "They saw me as half a person," fumes Kristin, 61, a former actress and model from Los Angeles. The white spaces on her calendar stretched out like a desolate road. Her phone rarely rang. Stung by her leperlike status, she complained to a woman who had been recently widowed. The widow had had the identical experience. Her advice: "Find new friends."

Women who lose a husband—whether through divorce or death—are plunged into a surreal landscape where they suddenly become outcasts. Their one or two best friends usually stick by them, but acquaintances and married couples who formed their larger social web mysteriously disappear. Newly single women sit home cradling the remote control while their married friends gather at parties and Saturday night movie dates. Certainly some women hold on to their couple friends, but it takes work.

It's a struggle for an ever-rising number of women. The number of divorced and separated women has more than doubled in the past three decades. In 2002, there were an estimated 12 million divorced women, compared to about 6 million in 1980, according to the U.S. Census Bureau. And the number of widows in 2002 tallied more than 11 million.

"When you're going through a divorce, you think, 'I cannot lose anything else,' and you find out, yes, you can," says one woman who was divorced after 35 years of marriage. That may also include beloved family members. Her sister-in-law and three brothers-in-law—who had become as close as her own siblings—froze her out after she left her husband. "It breaks your heart," she says.

Ironically, women who had antisocial husbands and kept friendships separate from their marriages didn't lose them after the divorce. In fact, sometimes the exodus of a wet-blanket spouse rejuvenated a relationship that may have cooled because a friend didn't like him.

Friends Bail on Widows

While widows are at first wreathed in more support than divorced women, the ultimate falloff of companions is often the same.

When Margie's husband was killed in a small-plane crash, many longtime family friends quickly fell away. At the funeral, ashen-faced friends of her husband, who had grown up with him in this rural South Carolina town, hugged her tightly and said, "If there is anything we can do to help, just call." They forgot to mention that their goodwill had an expiration date. "They were there for a little while, but then they quit calling, they quit coming by. They wouldn't even return my calls," says Margie, 41, an architect who runs her own firm. She understands people are tugged by their own lives. Still, she sensed it was more than that; she made people uneasy. "Friends weren't sure what to do with me now that I wasn't [part of] a couple anymore. It was a real odd feeling." She is grateful, though, for her two best girlfriends who check in weekly and a male neighbor who rushes over to her farmhouse at night with a flashlight if Margie hears a strange noise.

Tracey, a 37-year-old author from Poughkeepsie, New York, felt like a quarantine posting had been slapped on her front door after her young husband died of Hodgkin's disease. Invitations dried up, including one to a friend's annual holiday party. As the hostess explained in her most sensitive voice, "I didn't invite you because I thought you might feel uncomfortable. Everybody there was married."

"She might have at least asked," says Tracey. Sure, she might have been uncomfortable, but that doesn't mean she wouldn't have gone. "It was almost like I had a disease," she sighs.

Or a scarlet "W" emblazoned on her forehead. That's how Joanne, 51, felt when she swept into a bar mitzvah party at an elegant hotel—flushed with excitement to be at her first social event since her husband had died. Clutching her seating assignment card, she was stunned to discover her dinner partner at the table was the "other widow" at the event. "We were appalled. The last thing you want to do is be stuck with the other widow of the group because you feel like a pariah. Instead of seating me with my other married friends, she put us at a table where we didn't know anybody else."

Why do decent people behave like this? One reason simply

is that people feel most comfortable with others who have a similar lifestyle. Another is that most of us prefer not to think about the bad stuff that can happen. Divorced and widowed women remind us of the shadows that stalk all our lives and that a couple's happiness is as fragile as the crystal they received for their wedding. "It was too close for some of my friends," says Tracey. "It was like, 'Oh my God, it happened to you, could it happen to me?'"

She also knew married women worry that their freshly single friends may cast an amorous eye on their husbands (even though they usually have absolutely no interest). "They think I'm on the prowl ... or I'm looking for sex," observes Tracey with a rueful laugh. As a result, perhaps, socializing changed with the friends who stuck by her. "If I call up and say let's get a bite to eat, now only the wife will come."

Why Divorced Women Scare Friends

Married women often see divorced pals as even more of a threat to their marriages than widows. After all, the newly single friend could have designs on a woman's very own pot-bellied, balding Harold. As Rona's nervous pals blatantly asked her, "Would you ever go after a married man if you are feeling really lonely?" Rona, a striking, curvaceous, 49-year-old divorcée from Dallas, saw through this not-so-oblique question. "I would never demean myself to have anything to do with a married man, especially *your husband!*" she replied. She understands why they're worried, though. "A lot of married men in the community have hit on me. Some of these were husbands of women I love and respect. I'm going, 'Oh my God! This stinks!' The men said, 'If you are feeling lonely, I'll hold you, I'll take you out to dinner.

We can meet and just talk.' I said, 'I'd love to go out to dinner with you and *your wife.*'"

A divorced woman may also scare less-secure couples because she forces them to calibrate the stability of their own marriages. Carol, 34, saw that marital insecurity firsthand during a potluck dinner. When she announced to a female friend that she was leaving her husband, the woman and her spouse fled to the living room couch where they began a very public display of affection. Carol was aghast. "These people feel so threatened. They don't want it coming in their front door."

Yet another wedge between a divorced woman and her married friends appears when the friends go out with her ex-husband and his new girlfriend. Rona, for one, hates when her couple-friends have dinner with her ex. "They are being nice to the person who is hurting me. It feels like they are taking sides. It's almost like he gets away with something," she explains. She was particularly devastated when a couple she considered her closest married friends double-dated with her ex, Steve, and his new girlfriend. Rather than stew about it, though, she dealt with it head-on.

"I told my friends how betrayed I felt," Rona says. It gave them the chance to explain that going out with Steve and his girlfriend didn't diminish their love for her, which comforted her. It also didn't hurt when they confided that the double date was "the most uncomfortable night of their lives" and, even better for Rona, that they didn't like the girlfriend. "Those were the best words I could hear," Rona says with a laugh. Ultimately, she recognized that friends are not taking sides when they see her ex. "The reality means that they are trying to be a friend to both of us."

A Woman without a Country

If married acquaintances aren't sure what to do with newly single women, the truth is, the women aren't sure where they fit in, either. As a result, divorced and widowed women do their share of shedding friendships, which can feel like old shoes that suddenly pinch their toes.

When Tracey occasionally went out with couples, a new tension shimmered between them, as once-comfortable conversation topics now made her cringe. Seemingly innocent chats about family vacations, anniversary celebrations, or even bawdy sexual jokes felt like a slap. "It reminds you of what you don't have," she says.

Joanne was mightily annoyed when her friends complained how hard it was to manage their kids when their mates were out of town. Usually she did a silent burn. "But if I was feeling grouchy I'd look up and say, 'Well, at least he comes home!'" Joanne, a talent agent in Philadelphia, has been raising her young son and daughter on her own since her husband died five years ago. It grates that her friends aren't more sensitive to her daily existence.

"I felt more and more like I didn't belong," says Margie. That even included her church and the Sunday school class she had attended for years with her late husband. "Everybody else was there with a spouse. When a single person shows up, it makes for a really strained situation." Being with couples rubbed her face in the fact that she was alone. But singles clubs, "like bars without the alcohol," were also awkward; she didn't fit into that thinly disguised dating game, either. "I felt like a displaced person," she says.

"I had wonderful friends," says Angela, 50, a college professor in Vermont who recalls "the cards, letters, phone calls, hugs, flowers, and dinners" after her divorce. But after a while, she guiltily stopped returning her pals' phone calls. They jolted her back to still-raw memories. "People would always want to talk about it. I wanted to get on with my life. I wanted to move beyond that."

Tracey temporarily retreats from friends when she's overwhelmed by the chasm she sees between her life as a widow and theirs as a traditional family. She has also banished insensitive types such as the woman who was complaining about her husband. "You should be happy you don't have to put up with this anymore," she said. A stunned Tracey retorted, "I would give my right arm to fight with my husband again." End of friendship.

"I Can't Believe You Said That!"

You won't believe it either. Here are some of the amazing comments made to newly single women by acquaintances and friends.

1. "You'll really have to change your lifestyle!" said with barely concealed glee to a woman who was divorcing her husband, a doctor.

2. "I'm sure you must love having the house to yourself," said to a new widow.

3. "So, did you get a ton of insurance money?" also said to a new widow.

4. A widow received a call from a friend inviting her to join a table of people she was sponsoring for a charity ball. "Please bring a date," she said. "I'm sorry," said the grieving woman, "but as you know, I was recently widowed and I don't have a date." "Oh . . . you don't? Let's do it another time. I was just going to have couples at the table," the hostess replied.

5. Widownet.org offered this tidbit from a reader on its Web site: "A woman from Parents without Partners called to tell me when the next meeting would be and asked me how long I had been divorced. When I told her that my husband had died, she laughed and said, 'If it's any consolation, I wish my ex was dead.'"

Friends That Soothe

Thoughtful friends can make an enormous difference in the lives of their widowed or divorced pals. They certainly did for Shelly, 51, a widow in Los Angeles. Just before the one-year anniversary of her husband's death, friends asked what she wanted to do to honor the day. "I told them, 'Oh, nothing, don't worry about it.' But they wouldn't let me off the hook," Shelly recalls. Her buddies arranged a gourmet picnic in the park and presented her with a gift certificate for a massage, which they had scheduled for that afternoon. "They were telling me it was good to be indulgent on that day," Shelly says.

Friends continued to ease the way over all the painful hurdles in her bereavement. A month before her first Christmas as a widow, one pal realized Shelly's five-year-old daughter and eight-year-old son didn't have any way to buy their mom a present. So she secretly took them shopping for craft materials, then brought them to her house several times to make placemats and napkins they decorated with fabric markers. "I was overwhelmed with gratefulness," Shelly says. Then, for her first birthday after her husband died, friends threw her a surprise party. And on one Mother's Day, Shelly received an e-mail from a friend who recognized it was a tough day for her. She complimented Shelly on her terrific, well-adjusted children. "It's in large part to your wonderful mothering skills. Mark [Shelly's late husband] would be so proud of what you're doing," she wrote.

One of the most vital ways to help a newly single friend is simply by listening to her. That's why Shelly frequently checks in with two pals who are going through divorces. "I offer each of them a sounding board. I say, 'If you need someone to talk to, you can trust me not to take your confidence further than this room.'" And she doesn't expect a shard of reciprocity. "These are people who are having a really dark time in their lives. They don't need someone keeping score. When you're in crisis, sometimes it's all you can do to get yourself out of bed, and sometimes you can't even do that."

Women who have lost a partner also need people to pitch in with child care and the upkeep of the house. Tracey, the young widow from Poughkeepsie, appreciated neighbors who figured out what she needed and then did it without asking. The winter her husband died, for example, she woke up after the first snow and, with a sinking feeling, realized, "Oh, God, I have to shovel the driveway!" She peered out the window, but instead of mountainous drifts, she was stunned to see a clean driveway.

New Romance

Friendships may also fray when a divorced or widowed woman becomes romantically involved. Suddenly she's so caught up with her new beau that she can't find time for her old buddies. That can rankle pals who were there when *she* needed *them*. When Barbara's spouse abandoned her for another woman, Caroline rushed in to chauffeur Barbara's three kids, drop off dinners, offer a sympathetic ear. "I tried to help her through all the rough spots and the nastiness," she says. But once Barbara began seriously dating someone and eventually married him, Caroline, 51, was left behind. Barbara joined a new synagogue with her husband and made new friends. She was often busy with them when Caroline called to make plans. The two women still see each other, but it's not the same. "It makes me sad," says Caroline, wistfully recalling their former closeness.

"I will not be someone who drops her friends when a man comes along," declares Kristin, the former actress and model, who herself was swiftly dumped when a divorced friend fell in love with a new man. It still smarts when she recalls how the woman stopped returning her phone calls. "It says, 'You were a convenience when I was lonely; now that I'm not lonely anymore, see you around.'" Kristin has started dating someone, but that doesn't devalue her single female pals. "I will still call them and I will still want to get together with them," she promises.

Brake the Dump Truck

Another potential knot is a divorcée's or widow's unrelenting need to vent her anger and sadness, which can overwhelm even the most loyal friend. The friend wants her to move on, not understanding how long it takes to get through the mourning period.

"It takes an average of two years emotionally to get back on your feet," says Pam Tansey, a social worker who runs a marital crisis group for divorced women in the Chicago area. That can feel like a marathon even to supportive friends who may have trouble tolerating the grieving woman's pain. Sheila, a 33-year-old executive secretary from Indianapolis, thinks she may have driven some people away with her constant vitriol against her ex-husband. Now she wishes she had checked her complaining.

If you're the friend who's grieving, here are some signs of friend fatigue to look out for: she doesn't return your phone calls; you feel she's distancing herself; she says you should be over it. Some women just say, "Enough!" Lane jettisoned a divorced companion who nearly drowned her in an endless stream of self-pity, whether she bumped into her at the post office or met her for a sandwich. "I gave her two years to bitch and whine and complain and then I thought, 'If you can't move on, I'm moving on,'" she says. "It became boring. There wasn't anything you could do anymore. She wasn't healing. She was no longer likeable."

To preserve her friendships, it's essential for the widow or divorcée to tune in to people's limits. When Tracey began to sense her friends' discomfort, she'd say to herself, "'I've been talking about this enough. I should really change the conversation.' I started limiting how much I would say."

Joanne took to masking her grief at social gatherings. "You can say, 'I'm feeling really sad tonight,' but there is a point where you either have to leave the situation or change your focus. You don't want somebody sitting at a dinner party with a big, long face."

The fact is, some people just can't handle the powerful, raw emotions. One friend would dive off the phone while Debbie, a therapist from suburban Milwaukee, was still sobbing about her divorce. "Oh jeez, I gotta go," the friend would blurt. Click. When Debbie confronted her, the woman admitted she couldn't tolerate Debbie's anger and sadness, confessing those emotions were hard for her. She asked for another chance. Debbie gave it to her, but also understood "the limits of that relationship."

◦━✦━◦

SOLUTIONS

Landing in the Safety Net of Support Groups

There's a place where you don't have to conceal your grief and there's no time limit on crying or complaining. Support groups are unparalleled for a ready-made, empathetic audience willing to listen to the 100th story of your ex-husband's latest transgression and hold your hand while you cry for the ninth time that day. Here, single women no longer feel like aliens on the Planet Couples. They shed smiles that don't match their hearts in a place where, for an hour or two, they don't have to act strong.

Dos and Don'ts for Helping a Newly Single Friend

Here's how you can help a pal through her time of loss.

1. Listen without feeling that you have to comment or say something to make your friend feel better. Simply taking somebody's hand and touching her arm can be comforting.

2. Ask specifically what you can do to help as in, "Can I take the kids? Can I bring you dinner?" "We won't call to ask you. We feel like we're intruding on other people's lives. We can't even think straight about getting through the day, let alone tell you what to do. If you want to mow the lawn, don't ask us, just come and mow it," says Tracey, a widow from Poughkeepsie.

3. If you're discussing your husband with a woman who now doesn't have one, ask first if she's comfortable with the subject or if it's too painful for her.

4. Include your single friend in social activities, but understand if she's not ready. Invite her again in the future. "We work on our own grief schedules. We know what we're ready for," Tracey says. That also goes for dating.

5. If you're feeling overwhelmed or dragged down by your grieving friend's pain, gently set boundaries for what you can handle. You might say, "Right now I'm feeling overloaded. I understand you need to talk about this, so why don't we pick this up tomorrow?" Or, if she's repeating herself, you might say, "Remember we talked about this and you came to this conclusion?" suggests Ila Chaiken, a social worker who runs support groups at the Lilac Tree, an Evanston, Illinois, organization for women going through divorce.

Here's what to avoid when your friend is going through a loss.

1. Don't compare your loss to hers unless you've lost a husband.

2. Don't exclude someone just because you're uncomfortable about her loss.

3. Don't bash her ex-husband, no matter how much she does.

4. Don't give advice. Somebody going through a divorce or bereavement should have a therapist or a support group.

5. Don't say, "You'll find someone else." This is the last thing on a widow's or divorced woman's mind. She'll resent the suggestion.

Support groups spur recovery. Even if your friends are saints, you also need women who are struggling in the same muck you are. Unburdening your woes to a circle of caring women and listening to their stories is powerful medicine. It reassures you that you're not the only one suffering through this. And hearing how other women successfully cope provides you with tools for your own survival and the important belief that you, too, will resurface emotionally intact.

Since many of these groups are for women only, they're also a fertile place to mine new friends. Single women need some single pals. Married friends just can't understand how it feels to bolt awake at 3 A.M. wondering how you're going to manage on your own. But new companions are not so easy to find when you're so fogged in by grief you can barely make a phone call or are emotionally wobbly after a divorce. That's where support groups come in.

Groups can be either therapist-led or informal gatherings, such as a single parents' group at a grammar school. With social masks flung off and bone-deep experiences to share, bonds quickly gel between members. Some people become like extended family and gather at each other's holiday tables, a particular boon for older women who live alone. For example, some Chicago-area women, who met in a divorce group, celebrate Thanksgiving and Easter together. It's a comforting tradition for the women, whose adult children live out of town.

It may take time to find the right circle, though. Tracey walked into a widow's group to discover the other women were 20 to 30 years older than she was. "I was very uncomfortable because they didn't understand what I was going through. They said, 'Don't worry, you'll meet somebody.'" That was the last thing on her mind. She eventually found widows her age in a hospice bereavement group.

Nobody understands like someone who's been through it, as Margie, from South Carolina, discovered when she began an e-mail relationship with a woman who also had lost her husband in a plane crash. "When I told her what I was feeling, she knew exactly what I meant. There's part of the grieving process where you feel like you are losing your mind. Your thoughts don't make sense. It was very reassuring to know that what we were going through was normal." They e-mailed each other in the middle of the night when neither could sleep.

And someone who's lived through it knows that speaking the truth, not forced cheeriness, brings solace. Margie told her e-mail friend, "'I feel really sad for your two young daughters who are going to grow up not ever knowing what a wonderful man their daddy was.' She said I was the only person that said that. Everyone else said, 'Aren't you glad the girls are so young they won't have to go through all the grief?'"

Joanne, from Philadelphia, meets once a month with her "boo-hoo friends," a humorous name she assigns to two buddies whom she met four years ago in a bereavement group. One is a gay man who lost his partner, the other a married woman whose sister died. "In the beginning, we'd get together and we'd just cry our eyes out. You could be absolutely honest with these people and you didn't have to put on an act of 'I'm fine.' I could look at them and say, 'I can't bear it any more.' You never felt like you had to be strong and tough and pretend that things were fine when they really sucked. They would say, 'It does suck.' If we were in the mood, we would just wallow for the evening. Then we'd laugh in the middle and say, 'We are really bad tonight.' The next time we might not be so bad and have a happy dinner." Her boo-hoo friends also were tuned in to each other's emotionally raw times in ways that other people weren't. They sent each other flowers on the anniversary of their loved one's deaths.

For Joanne, these valued friendships have endured more than five years after her husband's death. Their connection has evolved to celebrate life after grief. Now dinners are less teary when they're together. "We're more likely to laugh and tease each other about new relationships—or the lack thereof!" she says.

But many women drift away from their bereavement friends as they grow stronger and more able to stand on their own. Some may not want to be reminded of that painful period. Others find their lives simply veer in new directions. Four women from suburban Seattle bonded like Krazy Glue when they all discovered their husbands, who were in a rock-and-roll band together, were cheating on them after performances. The furious wives were tight confidantes and social buddies throughout their divorces, catching movies and dinner together on lonely Saturday nights. But three years post-divorce, they see

Resources for Jump-Starting Your Social Life

If you're newly widowed, there are several resources available on the Internet that can connect you with other widows via e-mail lists and offer online support groups and information; www.widownet.org, www.griefnet.org, and www.youngwidowsandwidowers.com are just a few of them. WidowNet is an information and self-help resource written for and by widows and widowers. GriefNet is an Internet community of various support groups that is directed by a clinical grief psychologist.

To find a bereavement group, contact your local hospice, check the Yellow Pages, or visit the National Hospice and Palliative Care Organization Web site at www.nhpco.org. A local hospital or funeral home are other sources to check.

If you're newly divorced, you can contact your community's mental health center for divorce support groups. Or you can browse the Internet for support group sites such as www.divorcecare.org. DivorceCare offers nondenominational support groups sponsored by churches; its Web site lists locations. Parents without Partners has 400 chapters that provide educational and family activities; locate a chapter at www.parentswithoutpartners.org.

each other only occasionally. "We have gone on with our lives," says Fran, 51. "I got remarried, one girl moved downtown. Some went to work full time. It's not that they're not my friends anymore; they are just not my social life. I'm back with couple-friends."

Getting On with Your Life

Some newly single women may sit home, expecting everybody to call them, and be resentful when they don't. Not Rebecca. Her dining room table is often set for a crowd while she grills bratwurst in the backyard. Dinners are hardly gourmet, but since she was divorced last year her frequent entertaining has preserved relationships with married and single friends. "I'm comfortable with myself and with them, and, therefore, they're comfortable with me," she explains. "I like feeding them. I like hearing what's going on in their lives. It doesn't occur to me to worry that I'm here without a guy." As a single woman, she's still invited to plenty of parties with married couples. The women don't feel threatened by her, even though she's fit and attractive, with a mane of long, blonde hair. "I make a point of making the wife feel at ease," notes Rebecca, a 42-year-old Detroit fund-raiser with four school-age children. That means she always chats with the woman as much as the man and makes it clear she's interested in both their friendships. "I think a lot of women flirt with other people's husbands. I go out of my way to make sure she understands where I'm coming from. You can't lean emotionally on someone else's husband," she warns. "That's what girlfriends are for."

To retain some friends, especially those who were made through an ex-husband, a woman may have to discuss the new shape of the relationship—and maybe if they will even continue to have one. "There were certain people I wanted to fight for," says Rona, from Dallas. One was a woman who was vice president of a hospital where Rona's ex-husband was on staff. She and the woman had become close as they worked on fundraising together for many years. That chapter threatened to slam shut with the end of Rona's marriage. But Rona gutsily asked her, "Where do we go from here? Do we just say our good-byes and be thankful for this time we had together, or do you see me doing anything in the future with you?" The answer to the second question was a resounding yes. But until Rona brought it up, the woman hadn't understood how to shift their friendship to a different sphere. She now invites Rona out to lunch and sends her "I'm thinking about you" cards. Their tie might not have survived if Rona hadn't had the chutzpah to address the awkward situation.

Branching Out

Some women embrace an entirely new social network, where they won't be seen as half of a fractured couple but as whole women on their own. When Margie, the architect, shakily stepped into a women's Sunday school class at a new church, she saw the instant warmth in the mix of young and old faces looking back at her. "They accepted me as I am," she says. Within that group, she found other single mothers and began meeting them for dinner once a month to commiserate about the challenges of raising children on their own. She'd been worried that some of her kids' problems were the result of losing their father when they were so young. "It was a great reassurance to me that the stuff they are going through is not some strange psychological scarring. They're just normal preteen kids whose dad happened to die."

After Angela, the college professor, bought a condo in a new town, she plunged into adult education classes on ethics, real estate appraisal, and computers. There she hooked up with other single women for coffee or dinner after class, movies, and even vacation weekends in Maine. She also signed up for a gourmet dining club for singles. "It's fun discovering new people, sharing ideas, and not knowing everybody's story. There's no stereotyping," she says. She's thrilled to be unshackled from what she now sees as her suffocating married life. "I'm finding myself as a new person. We don't talk about high school activities and where the kids are going to college. We talk about politics and classes."

○━━━○

Being divorced or widowed dramatically alters and shears many friendships, a startling and painful surprise to newly single women. It's a punch in the stomach they didn't anticipate. They've not only lost a spouse, they've lost their social lives as they knew them. But being single doesn't sentence you to terminal loneliness. Support groups are an invaluable resource for women struggling to regain equilibrium and make new friends. And women who work to hold on to longtime social friends by calling them and affirming their friendships may see those relationships continue to thrive.

6

"I Can Work in My PJ's, but the Quiet Is Killing Me"

*Combating Isolation and Creating
a Work Community from Your Home*

NEARLY every afternoon at 5 o'clock, I glance at the clock and groan, "Oh, no, dinner!" It's always a surprise to me that I have to cook it yet again. Since I usually have nothing in the house except a couple of gray soy burgers entombed in freezer burn, I have to run to the store. Standing in a creeping checkout line every day isn't terribly efficient. Not to mention the fact that as soon as my hands touch the grocery cart, I assume the directional path of a hot-air balloon, a distractible, starving woman who hears the chocolate-covered marshmallow cookies whispering her name. I never get out of the store in less than half an hour. When I learned I could buy groceries online, it seemed like the perfect solution for a disorganized woman with bad shopping habits.

So I ordered food once a week and curtailed my grocery gambols. I saved time and money (tally cost of marshmallow cookies, Milky Ways, and other low-blood-sugar-inspired purchases). But I was miserable.

I missed Don, the platinum-haired produce manager, debating whether blueberries were truly the healthiest fruit—"or is it a bunch of propaganda?" I missed Robert's yarns about his pet canary, Pretty Boy, while he bagged my groceries. I missed bumping into my neighbors in the dairy aisle and discovering the best place to nab a middle school graduation dress. Because I worked at home, I rarely saw another human being all day. The grocery store was my social touchstone.

Okay, this is pretty sad. But working at home can be so isolating that even a trip to the grocery store becomes important. When a woman abandons a communal office to start a home-based business or become a free agent, it's a walloping adjustment. On Day One you'll discover that your fixed-up bedroom-cum-office is startlingly quiet. In downtown offices, women in stylish clothes are hustling, laughing, and ordering sushi for lunch. You, however, stare out the office window at the cardinal on the birdfeeder, brush the Danish crumbs off your pajamas, and can't understand why you feel so unmotivated.

When you leave a traditional workplace, you move out of "the neighborhood" where you may have some of your closest friends. You lose the countless exchanges that buoy you throughout the day—gossiping over Greek salads in the corner coffee shop, joking at the copier, stopping by your buddy's desk to ask about her kid's singing debut in the school musical. Now nobody knows you've got the flu unless you make a phone call to announce it. You're home alone. You also have to make your own lunch.

Sure, there are perks, which is why you did this in the first place. You can work in your nightgown, make personal phone calls without feeling like a felon, and be available to deliver a lunch box or Jack-in-the-Beanstalk costume to a certain for-getful second grader. But despite the luxurious new freedom, your spirits can sink faster than an Internet stock.

The symptoms of these plummeting spirits may be mysti-fying. "Women feel like they're moving in slow motion. They're easily overwhelmed. Everything feels hard," says Chris Essex, codirector of the Center for Work and Family in Rockville, Maryland. With some 3.25 million women now operating home-based businesses, legions of women are experiencing the emotional toll of isolation.

Chatting Up the UPS Man

Wendy didn't want any more days like the one where she had to nurse her baby at a client meeting after the nanny quit. So she ditched her job to launch her own business and nab more time with her kids. Now she runs a public relations firm from her home in Westchester County, New York.

But being home with the kids was short on stimulation. At midmorning her ear was tuned to the doorbell. "I really looked forward to the mail," laughs the 40-ish businesswoman. "I was schmoozing so much with the UPS man, he couldn't get on with his route." That's when she knew she was spending too much time alone. She missed the camaraderie of the office and the exchange of ideas that stirred her creative juices.

When you're isolated, lassitude may descend like a dense fog, as Barbara, 41, discovered when she chucked her job as an ac-quisitions editor for a publishing house to start her book pack-aging company in northern California. Sometimes she just stares out her office window at the horse pasture beyond or a hawk cir-cling the nearby lake. "It's lonely. I'm a very social person," she says. She spends a lot of time yakking to long-distance friends, her equivalent of "water cooler chat." And she grabs lunch at the local French bakery just to see other people's faces and hear their voices.

"If you start spending too much time by yourself, you start losing your people skills," says Carla, 42, who runs a virtual public relations agency for high-tech and life-sciences clients in Massachusetts. "When I don't see people for too long, I find my normally extroverted personality undergoes a great inversion. I don't want to leave the house. I can't get anything done. I get depressed. It doesn't take much to do it—just two days without seeing anybody."

SOLUTIONS

Your New Job: Finding Colleagues

Once you set up shop at home, you've got a second job: duplicating the gang you left in your former workplace. "It's not an easy void to fill," says Essex. "You really have to work hard at it. When it's not a natural part of the day, you have to schedule it." Women who feel pressed (and who doesn't?) think they can't afford to take the time. But they can't afford not to. Those seemingly insignificant daily interactions suffuse you with energy, good cheer, and fuel your productivity. "Recognize that you need it. Make it a priority to get it. Think of it as how you take care of yourself," Essex stresses.

She invents ways for workers to do exactly that. She worked with one group of women from a chemical company whose New Jersey office had gone virtual. They missed the routine day-to-day exchanges, the ability to stop by each other's desks to ask, "How was your birthday dinner?" or "How's your son? I heard he was sick." So she suggested the women pair up and check in with each other at the beginning and end of the day. They also met for coffee every Friday, a vital part of the plan. "There's a lot that's missed on the phone. There's body language, there's smiles, there's touching. They were missing face time," Essex says. (Interestingly, the men from the company weren't interested in the phone check-ins, though some would show up for the coffees.)

Anybody can set up a check-in with another work-at-home colleague. If you feel shy about calling everyday, e-mail is a less intrusive way to touch base. We all need to tell a friend when our 16-year-old son didn't roll in until 3 A.M. or that the puppy chewed up the cushions on the new couch. And we want to know all those things about our pals. These details tether us to each other's lives and make us feel safe and cared about.

Start a Professional Group

So how do you find new colleagues? One way is by starting an informal group of people in your profession. Mine meets once a month at a bakery where we chew over problems—personal and career—and laugh a lot, once earning us the glares of some elderly women diners who carped, "You sure are noisy!"

You bet. Perhaps it's an occupational hazard of our solitary profession that when we actually get together, we don't shut up. At one gathering, Suzanne tremulously confided that she is so overwhelmed by caring for her ailing mother and two young children that she hardly has time to work on her overdue book proposal. Later, Candy bit into a chocolate chip cookie and related a hilarious story of cleaning her messy house in record time before a last-minute television interview in her home.

This meeting is a sacred date on my calendar. For years I

had walked into this place and glanced enviously at the tables of women eating together. Now I'm among them, but it took some work.

I'd been wanting to start a group like this for a while, but I was scared. What if nobody wanted to come? What if they came but didn't like it? What if, what if, what if? Finally, I took the plunge. I invited one good writer friend and several women I liked but barely knew. They suggested other people. My group, and others like it, offers companionship, work problem solving, and a shot of encouragement when you're in a slump.

Starting a professional group is fairly simple. Network with people you know and ask them to suggest other names. Or place an ad in your local newspaper. Shoot for about six to eight people. Set a regular date—such as the first Friday of the month—to meet in each other's homes or a restaurant. Plan a loose agenda for each meeting—say, discussing some new research in your field. In my group, we read a chapter of a book or distribute an article to read before the next session. And allow plenty of time for socializing.

Get Out!

"Getting out is essential. You can learn things from other people," advises Wendy, who took pity on the UPS man and joined several business groups and her local chamber of commerce to meet new colleagues. She reaped social and business benefits such as finding a new graphic designer. She also began working two days a week for a public relations agency in New York City. "You remember how to dress up, how to look nice, how to interact," she says. "Getting into the city sparks my creativity. It gives me a total lift."

Being alone all day rusts your social skills. After a solitary week at home, I feel like the Tin Man before a squirt from the oil can. Carla, who works as a publicist from her home, avoids that rustiness by being as disciplined as a military strategist about scheduling some human contact every day. It's especially critical, she says, because she lives alone. "You have to have other people to anchor you. I have to physically see and talk to a person at least once a day." She crams her calendar a week in advance with dinner dates. With a blossoming second career as a science-humor writer, she gets her best ideas from being out with a buddy who might say, "Did you hear about the guy who grew a cow out of a side of beef?" Carla also organizes Diva Dinners, a quarterly gathering of stimulating women she knows.

Claudia, 37, who runs a Web design firm out of her home in Arlington, Massachusetts, also injects a slew of work-related socializing into her days. She organizes monthly pizza parties with other women entrepreneurs and their kids; the moms swap business tales while the kids play. For networking, she also serves on two nonprofit boards and is active in MIT's alumni events. She especially likes the contact with older women business owners, to see how they've balanced their careers and families.

Internet Colleagues

Using an exploding outlet for women who work at home, Wendy netted friends and colleagues in cyberspace through the

---

Resources

For bulletin or message boards, chat rooms, and e-mail lists for various work-at-home categories, check out Home-Based Working Moms (www.hbwm.com), Work at Home Moms (www.wahm.com), and Mothers & More (www.mothersandmore.org). Some Web sites also list women by geographic area so you can find colleagues in your neighborhood—and maybe grab that power lunch at the nearest park.

organizations Home-Based Working Moms and Work at Home Moms. "If you just got off the phone with a horrible person and you want to scream, there's an outlet. When you're working at home, who are you going to tell? The baby-sitter? The guy who's blowing the leaves on your lawn?" she asks.

Now Wendy e-mails and instant-messages her online colleagues to ask their advice on work problems and share the absurdities of home employment, such as the time a temporary employee arrived at her house toting two huge pillowcases of dirty laundry to throw into her washing machine. "They all got a really good laugh," she says. "They do their thing in their house and I do my thing in my house, but we're connected. With the Internet you can really get to know people in an intimate way. I think it's even more intimate than getting to know people who sit at the desk next to you." Still, she warns against revealing too much information, such as clients' names and fees, to people in the same profession. "And keep in mind the person you are talking to could be your next-door neighbor!"

⚬—⬥—⚬

Even though there's no one clocking the time you spend online and chat rooms can be addicting, don't let that stop you from venturing out of the house and into the world. Isolation can be a real party pooper. It dents your creativity, your energy, and your mood. The women who succeed at friendships while in their home offices know they have to work nearly as hard at lassoing new colleagues as they do at bringing in new business. Just leave your pink fuzzy slippers at home.

7

Good-Bye Power Lunches, Hello *Sesame Street*

❦

Breaking into the Mommy Circuit

MOMS who ditch their full-time jobs to stay home with their kids may suddenly feel like strangers in their own neighborhoods. And, in a way, they are. They may not know the names of the parents swirling around the grammar school doors when the bell rings or the moms giving "underdogs" on the park swings.

Knowing neighbors wasn't a priority, because career moms or moms-to-be were once working and socializing with another tribe eight or more hours a day. But now it matters a lot. They feel like they've got to crack these sealed circles of moms who appear to be such tight pals. "I feel like a kid standing on the edges of the schoolyard," lamented one newly at-home woman after she gazed enviously at a clutch of moms talking in the school parking lot. It yanks some women back to the bad old days of high school cliques, instantly husking career women of their confidence and baring their insecure teenage selves who anguished about their popularity.

Let's do a reality check. Sure, some of the moms are buddies. But the assumption that everyone has been secretly sworn in to an exclusive sorority—and YOU'RE NOT INVITED!—is dead wrong. Being "new" blurs the lens through which you view others' relationships. Because you feel out of it, you assume everyone else is in. In reality, the woman down the block may have just left her job, too. A growing number of moms are abandoning work to raise their kids. In 2002, 22 percent of married mothers with children under 15 stayed home to care for their families, compared to nearly 20 percent in 1994, according to the U.S. Census Bureau. When I moved into my town, I thought that any two women I saw just saying hello were close friends. It was only years later that I learned which women simply shared a carpool, which ones were superficially friendly because their kids played together, and which ones were as lonely as me.

A Stranger on My Own Block

"I didn't have time to make friends in my neighborhood," Kim, a former attorney for a Chicago law firm, says unapologetically. "I was busy working and raising my family." When she quit to stay home with her third child, she was understandably worried. "The nice thing about work is you have dozens of unimportant interactions that establish familiarity with people. It's hard to get those now," she says of her neighbors. She wonders, "How do you get a relationship to the next level where you can call up and say, 'Let's go to a movie or go shopping or play tennis, do something independent of our kids'? I haven't figured that out."

For Kim, 34, the isolation was especially troubling because her other friendships were dissolving. Old college pals and former work friends had either moved out of town or far enough away so that they saw each other only a few times a year. She wanted women who kept a finger on the pulse of her life and to keep hers on theirs. She wanted women she could ask why her kid was acting up and what color she should paint her kitchen when the yellow experiment didn't work. She wanted someone to stroll into her house and declare, "You need more gold!"

"There are lots of moms around, but that doesn't mean you can strike up a friendship with them," says Jennifer, 41, who suffered social whiplash after she left her job as director of a corporate tax department to stay home with her sons, ages 2 and 9. One week she was yakking with colleagues on the commute downtown to Denver, going out for lunch, then swapping office tales on the return trip. The next week she was sitting in a mom and tots class with her younger son feeling slighted by other women who didn't talk to her.

Former Colleagues Slip Away

Many women try to stay in touch with former coworkers, but the connection often slips away because they no longer share the camaraderie of the office. "They'd say, 'How's the baby?' but they didn't want to hear much," says Joanne Brundage, who left her job as a postal carrier in suburban Chicago when her first child was born. "You couldn't commiserate about the workplace. It became more and more difficult to have the same conversations we'd had because their daily reality was about working. My daily reality was trying to be in something other than pajamas by 2 o'clock in the afternoon."

The only glue to colleagues may have been the workplace and their proximity. "Slowly you begin to disengage. It's almost like a grieving process," Brundage says. Some of her female coworkers pulled away because her decision to stay home stirred up their own ambivalence about working full time. "I got the feeling it was too painful for them to maintain the relationship."

LOST IN MOMVILLE

Brundage's self-esteem took a hit when she turned in her mail satchel. "You don't realize how much your self-image is tied to the paid work you do. It hits you between the eyes. Being an at-home mom is incredibly different than being a working mom. It's a huge life transition," she observes. Others viewed her differently as well. "I had friends that asked me what detergent is best. It was tongue-in-cheek, but this was what they figured my life was about. I was so insulted." And when she chatted with strangers at parties, she quickly became a non-person. "You hit that 'What do you do?' question. As soon as I say, 'I'm home with my kids,' the light goes off behind their eyes because they think I have nothing to talk about."

If Brundage no longer felt linked to postal worker pals, she was horrified to discover neither could she relate to the moms on her block. "I tried to talk to them about how ambivalent I felt and that fell dead between us. They were so detached from the work world. They wanted to talk about recipes and diaper rash—and there's nothing wrong with that—but I was looking for intellectual stimulation."

Feeling lost, Brundage started FEMALE, a support group for former working moms like herself. From that first meeting in her living room, the group burgeoned into a national organization now called Mothers & More. "Everyone needs colleagues, whether you're home full time with your children or home and working in some capacity. You need to find other people who are having the same life experiences you are having," she emphasizes.

Unearthing Your Core Self

Being stripped of your longtime work identity may be unnerving at first, but it offers you a chance to excavate hidden parts of yourself. "It's figuring out who you are now that you're no longer in your job. It's like a sabbatical, taking a break from everything you've done before and looking deeply inward," says Martha Bullen, coauthor of *Staying Home: From Full-Time Professional to Full-Time Parent.* "You have to wait for the answers. It's almost a Zen thing. They will come but you can't rush it." It helps to delve into what you always loved or yearned to do but didn't have the time for, Bullen says. Your noncareer self will slowly emerge from the raw clay of your new life.

But until it does, don't try to justify your new status with explanations like, "I used to be the director of human resources, now I'm *just* home with my baby." "If you walk into a situation and act apologetic you get a different reception than if you say, 'I'm a home-based mom, and I'm lucky to be home with my kids,'" says Bullen. "If you're feeling insecure about your status, it would be hard to make new friends."

Keeping Your Head Down in the Mommy Wars

A decision to stay home may also spark skirmishes with moms who work. They may judge you: guilty for letting your brain atrophy! guilty for lollygagging around the house! They may envy you: What a cushy life! Must be nice!

Ann, a former CIA analyst, was pelted with verbal grenades after she had a baby and quit her job. Her friend, who had adopted a son, continued to work grueling 60-plus-hour weeks in her government job. During one chat, Ann innocently asked, "What have you been up to lately?" "Working!" the woman snapped. "*I* don't have time to do fun things!" "It implied that I just sit around and eat bonbons and watch soap operas," grumbles Ann. The woman seemed to blame Ann for her own stressful choices. Ann dumped her. "If every time you talk you feel bad, it's not worth calling anymore," she says.

But she can't protect herself from all the dings, like the comment by an attorney at one of Ann's parties who expressed relief that her husband, who was in the reserves, wasn't called to active duty. "What would I do as a military wife, just sit around and take care of my kid?" she sniffed. Or, as the woman in the park one Saturday asked, "You home?" "Yeah," Ann said. "Not me. I had a serious career I had to go back to."

Of course, at-home moms aren't innocents in this occasional battleground. Leslie Parrott, codirector for the Center for Relationship Development at Seattle Pacific University, is a marriage and family counselor, teacher, author, and national speaker. She is also the mom of two young sons. After her first son was born and she returned to work, "People were trying to imagine what I was robbing him of," says a bemused Parrott. "I don't know how you can do that," some women clucked disapprovingly. "Do you take him with you?" "How many classes do you teach?" "Do you write when he's taking a nap?" they quizzed her.

The fact is, you can't control anyone's reaction to your decision. Negative comments from either camp probably stem from women's doubts about their own choices. But don't fan the flames by dissing their choice or expounding about how important it is for a mother to be home. You have to watch your words more closely. "There is so much emotion invested in all this," warns Bullen. If your friend works 12 hours a day and you're thinking, 'How can she do that to her kids?' bite your tongue hard. Ditto if you wonder, 'Doesn't she go nuts staying home with her baby all day?' If flack from a good friend is endangering your relationship, discuss it in a neutral setting—sans children—in a way that doesn't attack her. One approach: "When you said my brain was going to rot, I was hurt. I feel like you are criticizing my decision to stay home." The bottom line is not to judge other people.

The more comfortable you are with your decision, the less rude comments will ruffle you. "For a long time, the more ambivalent I was, the more it created an emotional storm in me," says Parrott. But the jabs lost their power once she decided, "I will be the best mom when I am the most at peace. I felt called by both parts of my life. I found my own comfort zone and didn't try to please anyone else."

Don't Be a Doormat

One of the thorniest challenges for newly at-home mothers—especially those with infants—is shoving themselves out the door to meet people. Babies and young children tug at you nonstop. It's easy to sink like a stone into the bottomless sea of their needs. But that's when we lose ourselves. You no longer have an office job for socializing and feeding other parts of you. When you're at home, you need to make an effort to do that for yourself.

When I hired a sitter for my preschool-age daughter one evening for a rare dinner downtown, I bumped into an old friend from my pre-parent days. An ember of my old personality ignited, and suddenly I was an animated woman, laughing and chattering—a dramatic departure from my more somber personality of late. I was giddy at being reacquainted with my former self, whom I did not plan to lose again. "I have to get out more," I announced to my husband.

Elisa Morgan, the president of Mothers of Preschoolers International, a support group for mothers, says, "There's this universal myth that we're bad if we tend to our own needs." Envision a mom, she says, as a juice box with 12 straws piercing the box. "Moms do hit empty. We've got to understand that taking time for friends is not selfish; it's self-care."

∘━━━∘

SOLUTIONS

Breaking In

How do new at-home moms (or any at-home moms) make neighborhood friends? Even if you've lived in your town for a while, the challenge is the same.

Do make an effort to know your neighbors even if you don't envision becoming close. These are the women who greet you in the grocery store and who help in an emergency. They make you feel rooted. My next-door neighbor, Betty, generously loans me her car when mine is in the shop and offers me her refrigerator when mine overflows at Thanksgiving. When another neighbor's son came down with a fever at school, she called me to pick him up because she was stuck at work. None of us can manage it all on our own, and who'd want to?

Neighborhoods don't coalesce as naturally as they did in past generations, when most women stayed home full time with their kids. Achieving closeness these days takes the efforts of women like Kim and Emily, neighbors who single-handedly transformed their block in a Chicago suburb into the kind of place where women routinely knock on each other's doors just to say hi. "We worked hard on creating a neighborhood," says Kim. It doesn't happen by accident.

Although for several years Emily had lived three houses away from Kim, the attorney who felt isolated after she quit work to stay home with her kids, they didn't know each other. "I was lonely and bored," says Emily, also a former attorney home with a new baby.

When Emily, 41, greeted a neighbor at a park concert, the man — who lived across the street, for gosh sakes — stared back with a mystified look that seemed to say, "Who the heck are you?" She'd seen him mowing his lawn, but they'd never actually met. Emily decided to change all that. "I'm one of these hyperactive people," she admits. "I'm used to going 100 miles an hour." So she applied that energy to meeting neighbors, starting with a small coffee at her house for about eight women she knew only slightly. For the second get-together, Emily invited the whole block, tucking flyers into mailboxes up and down the street. This time her living room was a crush of women — some happily meeting each other for the first time. "I discovered there were some really cool ladies on this block," Emily says. That's when she met Kim. Gradually the two became friends and plotted ways to unite the moms on the block.

Once Emily's baby became more active — in other words, sticking her mitts in the coffee cake — she began organizing a ladies' night out at nearby restaurants every six weeks. Kim rallied their neighbors to plan an annual block party together; previously, only one woman had done it. By meeting regularly, they built in the small, accruing interactions that help people feel comfortable with each other and lay the foundation for deeper relationships. These are the exchanges that occur easily in school or in an office but are more scarce for women at home. At the party, they passed out name tags "so nobody would be embarrassed." Emily assembled a block directory with parents' and kids' names and phone numbers.

Kim's husband, David, wanted more contact with the men on the block, so he organized a rotating Friday night happy hour.

He knocked on doors and signed people up to take a night. Twice a month in the summer, a family hosts the outdoor fete that requires no more effort than ripping open a bag of chips, emptying a jar of salsa into a bowl, and serving soda and beer.

The upshot of Kim and Emily's efforts? On a block where many of the people didn't know each other's names, two years later the women knew not only each other but also everybody's husbands and kids. They could drop their children off at any house in an emergency or just sip an iced latte with a neighbor on a sultry August afternoon. Kim recently banged on the screen door of a woman down the street to ask what she was wearing to a going-away party for a neighbor. Once they settled on the proper dress, the neighbor remarked that today was the last day of camp for Kim's daughter. It was both an ordinary and extraordinary moment for Kim. "She knew enough about my life to say that to me. It's really nice to have that sense of connectedness." Now when she mentions her address to other women in her suburb, they enviously say, "That's the best street to live on!"

Emily discovered intimacy can pinch, though. "I've gotten to know people who have really hurt my feelings," she says. One group of women, whom she'd always included in her coffees and her Christmas card-making party, didn't invite her when they organized a weekly Bunco game. Then, when they called her to be a substitute, she discovered she was "the fifth resort for a sub for their regular game." Ouch. She already had plans, but she wouldn't have gone even if she were free. "I was a last resort and nobody wants to feel like that," she says.

Then she discovered a woman was gossiping about her and her husband. "It's like a workplace after a while," says a disappointed Emily. "There's the politics and this person talking about that person. But I'm not getting paid to put up with this."

Resources

If there aren't a lot of at-home moms nearby or you haven't seen any glimmers of friendship from the women who are, branch out with these national groups. Remember, it takes time to feel comfortable in a new group. Give it at least two or three visits to decide if it's the place for you. A few questions to consider: Are you greeted warmly or ignored? Do you feel heard in the group? Do you have things in common with the other members?

If one group doesn't fit, try another! Here are just a few:

With 175 national chapters, Mothers & More (www.mothersandmore.org) has monthly meetings, play groups, and moms' nights out as well as an active virtual community.

If there isn't a branch of the National Association of Mothers' Centers (www.motherscenter.org or [800] 645-3828) in your area, the Levittown, New York–based group will help you launch one and provide group facilitation training.

Mothers of Preschoolers International, or MOPS (www.mops.org or [800] 929-1287), is a Christian-based group that is open to all moms and has 2,600 chapters nationwide. Every meeting breaks up into small groups to help women get to know each other.

At one ladies' night out, when Emily complained about her husband's lack of help at home—a time-honored topic of conversation when women get together—a neighbor sniped, "Well, Emily, if you're done bitching about your husband, let's talk about something else." Disheartened and bruised, Emily stopped organizing the outings. What was the point, she wondered, if she kept getting kicked in the shins?

Now, months later, she misses them. And she's had an epiphany. "I've taken things way too personally. I need to loosen up and lighten up. People are going to be people [with all their foibles]. Your world closes in when you're not working. Little things that I would have laughed off or wouldn't have registered before take on more importance than they should."

So she's going to plan another party. "We can still have a

good time even if we don't see eye to eye. We'll see what happens," she says hopefully. Some neighbors suggested she just invite the women she likes, but Emily doesn't want to hurt anyone's feelings. "I'm going to be the bigger person. I'll give it another stab."

Emily's experience reflects the dustups inevitable in any group of women—or people, for that matter. Some women are catty and untrustworthy. More are warm and genuine. It will never be perfect.

In the meantime, Emily tries to focus on the good. And there has been plenty of that, particularly her friendship with Kim. They stalk yard sales together and meet Saturday mornings to load up on flowers and tomatoes at the farmers' market. Kim has also been her guide for everything from doctors to landscapers.

Lots of new at-home moms are feeling like aliens in the park. They may not realize it, but they have plenty of company right in their neighborhoods. Many women would like to get to know each other better. So knock on some doors and plan a coffee. Volunteer often for activities at your kid's school and for the PTA. Try a chapter meeting of a moms' group. Over time, at the very least you'll discover some new peers and form a web of acquaintances, maybe even some friends. A new companion may be as close as three doors away, as Kim and Emily discovered.

8

Ripping Up Your Roots
and Sinking New Ones

⚬━━━⚬

Finding Friends after a Move

EVEN women who hopscotch with their families across the country every few years can't escape the emotional wrench of starting over. It's overwhelming to seek and build friendships in a town where you don't know a soul, save your real estate agent.

Once the kids are registered for soccer, the name of a good pediatrician procured, and the spices alphabetized in the rack, that's when you have to face the music of your newly untethered life. "Starting over stinks. Sometimes the loneliness feels open ended and scary," says author Leslie Levine, who moved to a Chicago suburb from Rochester, New York. She reminds herself, "I'm lonely now. This is going to pass."

But until it does, you feel like a ghost floating through town who doesn't leave any footprints. No one sees you because no one knows you.

A Disappearing Act

"I'm invisible!" laments Carlene, 44, who moved back to the United States after a 14-year stint in Hong Kong with her family. Overseas, she had been cozily enveloped in a chrysalis of American expatriates, where everyone knew her as a teacher at her kids' grammar school and a fixture at the tennis club. Now she sits alone in the stands at her daughter's soccer games in suburban Detroit. Her children quickly made new pals at school, but Carlene felt she was wandering through a labyrinth, crashing into one dead end after another.

She joined a choir and a tennis group, but those weekly meetings never yielded more than superficial hellos from other members. Some days she felt so melancholy, she couldn't rouse herself to leave the house. "I'll have three or four bad days. I won't be able to accomplish much because I feel like I'm moving through molasses," she sighs.

Many women are suffering similar pangs of estrangement. Some 43.4 million people moved to a new home between 1999 and 2000, according to the U.S. Census Bureau, with 8.4 million relocating to another state. While out-of-state moves are the most traumatic, even relatively short hops from the city to the suburbs can cause disconnection.

A Confidence Jolt

When we're unplugged from friends, we may devolve from our once confident selves and begin to question our likability. My self-assurance plummeted after I moved to Dallas. When I prepared to entertain my new next-door neighbor, my hands were as icy as if I were going on a blind date. The stakes seemed so high. When she didn't touch the feta cheese dip I'd concocted,

I fretted that it was too exotic and I'd blown it. Even though a bevy of devoted pals may live several states away, the transition between leaving old relationships and bridging new ones can knock us off balance.

It's not surprising that severing old ties is so traumatic. "Connections are the core of women's lives," says Judy Jordan, a clinical psychologist, author, and researcher at the Stone Center, part of the Wellesley Centers for Women at Wellesley College in Massachusetts. Without them, we're like a tripod with a missing leg. "That yearning for connection is so strong that when you move and are experiencing the loss of old friendships, women often feel a lot of grief, a lot of sadness, and a lot of regrets," Jordan says. It's critical to stay in frequent touch with the pals you left behind. They'll ground you and remind you that you are lovable.

After a move, you're drained by the constant effort of introducing yourself, reciting your story, and convincing people that you're worth getting to know. "You always have to put your best foot forward," explains Andy Schweitzer, a social worker who has led support groups for newcomers at the Women's Exchange in Winnetka, Illinois. "You can't relax the way you can with old friends. There's much more of a sense of presenting yourself to the world. There is real pressure that goes with that."

Without outside companionship, married women demand more from their husbands. "He has to be your husband, your best friend, and your acquaintances. It's hard for a person to fill all those needs—in fact, basically impossible," says Schweitzer, who experienced this herself when she relocated from New York to a Chicago suburb. She recalls hungrily pouncing on her husband at the end of the day. "I wanted him to feed me some tidbits from any conversation he had with anybody."

Women who work outside the home may have a slightly

easier time settling in than those who stay home because they can mine the office for friends. Still, even that's no guarantee of companionship. Colleagues may be polite, but won't necessarily trip over themselves to embrace you. Or you just may not have much in common with them beyond the job.

Glacial Progress

Breaking into a new community is often agonizingly slow. Old, established cities—where women still hang out with their friends from kindergarten, not to mention their extended family—can seem impenetrable. Places teeming with recent transplants, like Atlanta, Dallas, Denver, Phoenix, or Seattle, are more hospitable because lots of people are trolling for new relationships. So are new subdivisions, where everyone is unpacking their moving boxes, watering their sod, and looking for friends.

When Sharon's moving van pulled into a 300-year-old historic town in suburban Philadelphia, it wasn't the unseasonable March snowfall that made her shiver. It was the frosty welcome from longtime residents, a painful contrast to the easy embrace of her former neighbors in the San Francisco Bay area. "This is an incredibly difficult area to break into. The longstanding residents have no interest in meeting anyone else," says Sharon, 41. "They've been here for generations; they have old school ties, they have church. You get the cold shoulder if your family hasn't been here for 200 years."

Little did I know that when I rapidly nabbed good friends in Dallas—the first time I'd ever lived outside Chicago—my experience was the exception. Why had it been easy there and so hard when I moved back to the town where I grew up? I couldn't figure it out. Then it hit me. In Dallas, most of my friends at the newspaper were culled from a wave of new hires.

It was akin to freshman year at college—except we were in a newsroom navigating a new job and, at the end of the day, searching for someone to join us for an icy Lone Star on a steamy night (they were all steamy nights). Toss in the fact that we saw each other every day in a high-pressure atmosphere, and you had the essential ingredients for rapid bonding.

But this lucky confluence of circumstances is rare. Usually we land in a place where women are too wrapped up in their own lives to extend themselves to a newcomer. If somebody does invite you over, it's often a one-time gesture, not an overture to friendship. "You have lunch together and they say, 'Welcome to the neighborhood,' and that's the last time you see them," says Jordan. "All the slots are filled."

Plotting Your Strategy

That's why you need a well-honed plan. "By having a strategy, you feel empowered as opposed to 'poor me,'" says Chris Essex, codirector of the Center for Work and Family in Rockville, Maryland.

But my own strategy stunk. Becoming a room mom at my daughter's school exposed me to only a small number of women; the yoga class I took was taught in a silent, meditative atmosphere that didn't encourage chatting. The mothers of my daughter's friends and I didn't have much in common, so that riverbed was dry. I couldn't see how to bust out of my little corner of the world.

Neither could Francesca, 30, a former newspaper editor, who practically lost count of the women she tried to befriend after she moved to Savannah, Georgia, from San Diego. She invited women out for lunch and coffee, hosted backyard barbecues and Christmas and Easter dinners. Everyone was happy to come over and denude her tasty buffet table, but no one invited her back. "It's closed me up. I don't want to put myself out there anymore, I've been burned so many times," she says.

○━━━○

SOLUTIONS

Focusing the Hunt

Francesca and I could have learned a thing or two from Sharon and several other women who have burnished the techniques of making new friends to a gleaming art. Some of it is knowing where to hunt—like a pig snuffling for the elusive white truffles in the forest. The other secret is knowing how to unearth them once they're in sight. Pursuing someone too ardently—a real danger when you're lonely and needy—can scare away candidates. Here's a look at how they did it.

SHARON: SEEK OUT OTHER NEWCOMERS

Although Sharon's neighbors weren't lining up with plates of brownies to welcome her, she wasn't miserable or lonely for long in her new town. She had already discovered the express lane to new companions when she'd first moved to the San Francisco Bay area from Chicago, before embarking to Philly: join a national women's group where there are sure to be other newcomers.

For her, that group was Mothers & More. "You can really get into quick, substantive conversations. I hate chitchat. These women are on the same wavelength," says Sharon. So before Sharon relocated to Philadelphia, she contacted the local Mothers & More chapter there to get the lowdown on good school districts, check out where members lived, and locate a dance class for her daughter. "It cut out so much anxiety and confusion," she says. She and her husband even bought a house near the chapter headquarters. Once there, she forced herself to go to every meeting and program, knowing that face time is critical. She also became a member of the board, and the extra meetings brought her closer to active members.

But when she joined the Newcomers Club, an organization for women fresh to an area, Sharon didn't immediately spy any soul mates. She didn't feel compatible with certain factions who preferred to talk about shopping and hair. Eventually, though, she discovered like minds in the book discussion group. It was a lesson in how to discover a niche within a larger club that may not be a perfect fit.

"Without the clubs, the move would have been miserable," Sharon says. Within six months she had four new pals—which, as women who have moved know, is like winning the friendship lottery. It often takes much longer.

That's not to say Sharon is doing handsprings. Yes, she has companions. Yes, she lives on a winding road with 18th-century houses, where horses and sheep graze in a nearby field. But her roots there are still wispy strands, not the gnarly ropes that once tied her to Chicago and California—not yet. She knows it takes time for those roots to thicken and grow.

Jenny: Treat It like a Job

Jenny doesn't collect a paycheck, but this at-home mom considers herself fully employed after the moving van pulls away, which it has done many times in England and once in the United States. "I treat meeting people as my job. I do it with military precision," says Jenny, 34, a lively British native who is so engaging you want to meet her for coffee after a 2-minute conversation. Like Sharon, she also delves into a collection of women's groups and does not permit herself to sit home. She's weathered bruising rebuffs, but also savored flourishing relationships. The evidence of her success: the good-bye party thrown by her mournful friends and neighbors when it was time to pack up yet again for a new destination when her husband's company transferred him. "I say the glass is half full. I look forward to going on to new things. I see it as an adventure," she says. Here's her technique.

How she nails down a date: "If I've met somebody and they say, 'We'll have to have coffee,' and if I've zeroed in on them as a potential friend, I would get a date to have them over then and there. I'll say, 'What are you doing tomorrow?' Everybody says, 'Let's get together,' but they never do. If they won't be pinned down, then you know it's not worth pursuing."

A humiliation-free way to gauge someone's interest: "I phone people when I know they're not going to be there and leave a message. I'll say, 'I thought we might get the kids together. Please give me a call.' If you phone them when they're home and they're not interested, it's awkward. They have to think of an excuse. If you leave a message and they never call, you know they never intended to do it anyway. When you bump into the person who apologizes for not calling back, say, 'Oh don't worry about it. It's really a busy time of year.'"

What she tells herself after she's been rejected: "I was disappointed but I wasn't necessarily offended. I'm sure some people I wanted to be friends with probably had enough friends. It's not that they didn't like me. I'd say, 'Her loss.' You have to move on. Over time, you realize the people who don't call you [back] ultimately would not have been your good friends because there wasn't a connection for them. The ones who do call you are the ones you get on the best with."

Her door is always open and she hopes yours is, too. "I'm not shy about knocking on the door and asking to borrow something [as a ploy to meet a neighbor]. The next day I'll be back to return the cup of sugar and see if someone invites me in."

CHRIS: THE STRATEGIST

With an older teenage son, Chris Essex's days for meeting women through school activities are long over. Nor does she have ready-made colleagues; since she moved back to Maryland, she works at home as a corporate consultant for work and family issues. So now Essex sails through her day like a keen-eyed fisherman, always on the lookout to reel in a potential girlfriend. When she encounters someone she likes, she plots ways to convert her to a friend. She's also proactive—once forming a professional group with 40 people that both provided a useful network and enlarged the pool for potential pals. She admits her approach demands a lot of energy. "I feel like I've spent the last two years screening people for friends," she says. But it's paid off.

Here's the approach that's netted her new companions in moves to several different towns. "You have to get resourceful," Essex stresses. "I've learned I need to make the first move, because it's *my* need. They don't know that I'm feeling isolated and lonely." Park your shyness at the door.

Timing is everything: One morning on a fitness walk in her new neighborhood, Essex noticed a knot of women waiting with their kids at the elementary school bus stop. Her son was in junior high, so she wouldn't have been a natural member of this "little network of social support." While most of us would stare enviously as we power-walked by and shrug, Essex began timing her morning walk to bump into the women just as their kids were boarding the bus. "I'd hang out there and kibitz for a while. You have to be strategic."

Where to Meet People

Try these places and activities to expand your social circle.

1. Check your church, synagogue, or community center for friendship or discussion groups.

2. Inquire about book clubs at your local bookstore and library. If they don't have an existing group, ask about starting one.

3. Volunteer. Some towns have volunteer centers that can match you with organizations. One woman made terrific pals as the organizer for her suburb's July 4th festivities. Another forged a new friendship group from women she met planning fundraisers to feed the hungry. All those frequent meetings fertilize new relationships.

4. Try a memoir writing class. Look for one in adult education classes at a community college or local university or through ads in the newspaper book section. People sharing their life stories are easier to get to know. Check out other classes that intrigue you, whether it's knitting, cake decorating, sailing, gardening, pottery, acting, or stand-up comedy. Adult education programs at community colleges, universities, and park districts are good sources, but also try yarn shops, art and drama schools, and a botanic garden. Be resourceful.

5. Visit www.newcomersclub.com for a worldwide directory of clubs and

The chance meeting: When Essex stabbed her fork into a Caesar salad at a gourmet takeout counter, she noticed a tastier lunch of grilled chicken on the plate next to hers. "That looks good!" she commented to the woman. As they began to chat, Essex learned that the woman's daughter was home on a short maternity leave, and she offered to send her some postpartum information. Later, when Essex called to tell her she was faxing the material, she asked about getting together for lunch. "I knew she was really busy. I said, 'You name the place, time, and day.'" At the lunch, the woman, who owned a real estate company, complimented Essex on her outfit. "Shopping is my hobby," Essex organizations that welcome you to a town, such as New Neighbors and Welcome Friends. If your area isn't listed, contact the local chamber of commerce to see whether there's a women's club for new residents.

6. If you're a mom, there are several Web sites to help you connect with a local group: www.mothersandmore.org, www.motherscenter.org, and www.mops.org.

7. The American Association for University Women has nationwide chapters that offer, among other activities, discussion, book, movie, and dining groups. Locate a local chapter at www.aauw.org.

8. The Red Hat Society has chapters around the country devoted to tea parties and a good time for all. The only requirement is a red hat and a purple outfit if you're 50 and older, a pink hat and lavender clothes if you're younger. Its Web site, www.redhatsociety.com, lists chapters (and whether they're open to new members) and offers a guide for starting your own. It also has a national convention and a newsletter.

9. Check out aerobic, spinning, or kickboxing classes at the YMCA, YWCA, JCC, or neighborhood health club.

10. Buy a dog or walk a neighbor's dog. It's a great conversation starter with other dog owners. See if there's a doggie park in your area by asking around or checking www.dogpark.com, a national dog parks Web site.

confessed with a guilty laugh. "Mine, too! I don't like to admit it," said the woman. They discovered they both loved to outlet shop and made a date to hit the mall. Now it's their routine.

Nudging the decorator: After Essex's encounter with the real estate agent, she purposely stopped to pick something up from her decorator, a woman with whom she'd hit it off. "I said, 'I'm so excited! I made a new friend today.' I thought if I let it slip that I'm looking for friends, she might pick up on it. She said, 'Aren't I a friend?' I said, 'We've never had lunch together. Would you like to be my friend, because I'd like to have you as a friend.' Now we're best buddies." They meet two Saturdays a month, first fitness walking, then grabbing their ritual break-fast—egg white omelets with tomatoes, onions, and mush-rooms—before heading off to browse antique stores.

The friendly saleswoman: Essex found herself laughing a lot with a saleswoman at Bloomingdale's whom she met when she was shopping for china. When she returns to buy the dishes, Essex plans to hand the woman a business card and say, "We had a lot of fun [picking out plates]. If you ever want to get a coffee or have lunch, let me know. Here's my phone number. I'd love to get together."

Walking partners wanted: To find walking partners after a move to northern California, Essex stashed paper strips with her phone number in her pocket and diaper bag. "I asked every-body," she says, figuring she passed out 50 slips of paper before she assembled walking buddies four days a week.

The nervous old friend: When she moved back to Rockville, Essex remembered an old friend. "I'm needier than she is. She was worried that I was going to bug her and that she was going to feel guilty if she didn't include me in everything. I said, 'Let's agree we are in two different stages. I'm needy, I admit it. And I'll be sensitive that your dance card is full.'" The friend hesitated to invite Essex to her annual New Year's Eve party because she hates to mix friends and didn't want to feel re-sponsible for her. "I said, 'Why don't you give us a try? If it feels burdensome, we won't do it again.'" Essex has been invited back to the party five years running.

LESLIE: PATIENCE, A TOUGH HIDE, THEN THE PAYOFF

After resettling in two new towns, author Leslie Levine's phi-losophy has helped her weather rebuffs and keep trying. "You have to be willing to say to yourself [if you get rejected], this person is really busy or they have all the friends they need right now," she says. "There are disappointments, and you have to live through those. The person who doesn't become your friend today may become your friend in a year. You can't give up and you can't put yourself down."

Sometimes you go out with someone and think you clicked, but the other person doesn't, Levine says. "You have to realize there are things you don't know about other people." The woman who seems standoffish may be shy, or she may be going through a personal trauma.

Keep in mind that it's usually not about you. But sometimes it is, and that's okay. Not everyone is going to love you. After two years of "casting a wide net" and watering the seeds of new relationships, Levine knew she had moved beyond the sapling stage with new pals when her mother-in-law died. The phone started ringing. Friends and neighbors delivered dinner. Then they arrived on her doorstep toting coffeemakers and coffee cake to 'sit shiva,' a Jewish tradition for paying condolences after a death. Her house was full. So was her heart.

Finding a Group That Fits

Who hasn't inched gingerly, heart hammering, into a gathering of strangers, gaped at the sea of unfamiliar faces, and wondered how soon you can bolt and whose idea was this anyhow?

It's not fun in the beginning. You have to force yourself out the door when it's a lot less threatening to stay home and rearrange your knickknacks. Here's how Sharon triumphs over her nerves. "I give myself a pep talk and say, 'You need to get out and meet people. They're not going to go out and look for you. This is something I have to do for myself.'" The toughest part once she gets there is trying not to act too desperate and blurting out, "I need some friends!"

Maybe you'll connect instantly with other women at your first meeting (*"Jane Eyre* is my favorite book, too!"), but it will probably take longer. "Hang in there two or three times," advises Judi Geake, the executive director of the nonprofit Women's Exchange in Winnetka, Illinois, who has organized and presided over hundreds of women's support and discussion groups there. It's natural to feel uncomfortable at first. While you may quickly size up the extroverts, quieter types take longer. The person who eventually became one of my best friends in Dallas was so shy she barely spoke to me for weeks, even though her desk was next to mine.

Geake offers the following suggestions to improve your success rate when you test a group.

Look for a smallish group that is new or has an influx of new members. "It's harder to join an ongoing group because people have already formed connections. It will take longer to feel part of it. Established groups have a language all their own and a common history. It's like going to your husband's high school reunion," Geake says.

Indeed, when Jenny, the spirited British woman, ventured into a long-running play group with her 2-year-old daughter, she was a perennial outsider. "They would say, 'Hi, how are you settling in?' but nobody really included me in a conversation. They spoke about things that were familiar to them and not to me at all. I think it was pretty rude. After a while I broke in but it took me three or four months." But the fact that it took her so long was probably a sign that these women were not going to become Jenny's close friends, which they didn't.

Contrast that to Jenny's experience at the drop-in baby-sitting center where fresh faces always appeared and everybody played on a level field. She introduced herself to the new recruits and instantly liked one woman with a wicked wit, similar to her own. "She made me laugh. I knew that we would be friends. She said the same thing about me. I had that rapport with her."

Are you on the same page as the other members? If you're a corporate vice president and they're passionate at-home moms, you may not have much in common. Are they dressed like you? It's superficial, but clothes are shorthand for lifestyle and attitudes. One woman knew she was in *the wrong place* when she arrived at a Newcomers Club meeting in blue jeans and trendy platform hiking boots. She was appalled to see everyone else—who looked to be ten years older than she was—wearing Christmas-motif sweaters. "They looked at me like I was an alien," she says with a shudder.

Do you care about protecting wildlife, feeding the hungry, or reading great women authors? Seek a group whose focus matches your interests, which means you will have at least one thing in common.

When women reveal their deeper selves, bonding accelerates. Even so, in such groups—like book, parenting, or spirituality circles—it may take six to eight weeks before relationships start to gel.

Do you feel heard in the group? Do people take the time to listen to you? Is there pressure to conform or can you be yourself? Do you feel safe sharing personal information? Do you relax and enjoy the company of these women, or are you on edge? Do you enjoy hearing the other women's stories as well as telling your own?

Are you greeted warmly or ignored? Do people make an effort to include you?

Keep trying. A college professor in a new town felt unwelcome in a women's discussion group at her church, so she pressed her reluctant husband to come with her to a couples group there. Bingo! At that meeting, she met a circle of women who were to become dear friends.

A Blueprint for Your Own Newcomers Group

You're sure you're the only one who feels like an alien in this place. It's not true, of course, but that's what you believe after a move. A newcomers support group offers reality checks to your temporary delusions. "It's the antidote to the loneliness of thinking you're the only person going though this. There's that feeling of isolation when you look around you and it seems like everyone else is settled and happy and has their little niche in the world and you don't," says Andy Schweitzer, the newcomers support group leader.

This is a safe place to pry off the smiley mask ("I love it here and everything's terrific!") and be genuine ("This is so hard!"). Here you discover that other women are also despairing over whether they'll ever belong. Schweitzer says her group's mantra was, "'It just takes time.' We repeated it over and over."

You can assemble your own group by checking with the local schools or PTAs for new families in the area, posting signs in the library, and advertising in the local paper. Here's the weekly agenda for the group at the Women's Exchange. Shoot for eight women (but fewer is okay), and plan on meeting once a week for at least six weeks. If you enjoy each other, the group may even stay together and shift its focus to talk about other topics.

1. Introductions
2. Tell us something different about yourself that you did not tell us the first time. Discuss the meaning of identity.
3. Relate something you left behind in the place you came from: a job, an activity, a relationship, an identity. Dis-

cuss grieving over lost relationships, lost identity, and loss
of familiar surroundings.

4. How did the move affect relationships with your chil-
    dren, spouse, friends, and parents? Which ones are now
    more difficult? Which are easier?

5. Discuss an important activity in your life before you
    moved. How could you recreate the feeling that activity
    stirred in you?

6. What have you learned from the experience of moving
    or starting over?

◦——✦——◦

Moving tears us from the people we love. Then we have to
buck up and build an entire web of new friendships. It's less
overwhelming if you have a well-honed strategy. That means
venturing into groups and classes even when it feels scary. But a
future friend may also be the saleswoman at Bloomingdale's
who helps you pick out your new china. Take some risks and be
open to all the possibilities.

9

Roadblocks to Friendship

THE chocolate cake in the cooking magazine immediately snared me. The triple layers of dark devil's food—my favorite—were glazed with a rich, fudgy ganache. I'd been craving chocolate cake. I could almost taste it. Maybe I'd share it with my family, maybe not. Then I noticed the lengthy list of ingredients, including an artisan chocolate that had to be specially ordered from a catalog. The recipe was complicated—carefully melting chocolate in a double boiler and whipping egg whites. Way too much trouble. Even though I knew it would be delicious, I turned the page.

New friendships can feel like that. You're drawn to the picture—a woman who, with her spicy joke, generous smile, or Grateful Dead T-shirt, radiates possibilities. A jolt of connection strikes. She's someone you could really like. But you tally the cost—emotional energy, complicated dance steps, and patience for the unrushable process (you call her, she calls you, you call her—are we friends yet?)—and you take a pass.

If you invite her out for coffee and she rejects the invitation, you risk being nicked. If she accepts, you chance revealing precious parts of yourself that may return to haunt you if she's loose-lipped or the relationship sours. You expose yourself to pain even if the friendship thrives. Intimate relationships are messy; the most glorious ones still serve up occasional misunderstandings or disappointments. And it may not work out.

I sport a few surface scars from fledgling friendships that cantered ahead, then faltered on a loose divot—sometimes my fault, sometimes not. Most, I think, were not meant to be. But the failed start-ups nagged at me for months. Ultimately, several "chances" I took worked out very well, indeed. The women became terrific friends. You just never know.

There are infinite reasons—and excuses—not to seek a new pal. Shyness may hobble you. A hurtful childhood experience with girlfriends may have trampled your confidence or trust. A difficult childhood relationship with family may also hinder you. Then, some women are convinced no one will ever match their old buddies from another life, so why even try? It's easier not to venture beyond your limited circle. But at what price? An infusion of new blood means fresh ideas and adventures. Life with the same old crowd can become predictable and pale.

The Struggle of Shy Women

For much of her life, Rebecca, 44, has watched other people schmooze, yak, and mingle while she hugs a folding chair or stands awkwardly on the sidelines, like a wallflower at a high school dance. She studies other people's seeming ease with each other, puzzling over what they exude that she doesn't, searching herself for fatal flaws.

"Maybe I don't have magic with people. Maybe I'm not a good enough conversationalist. Maybe I'm too serious. Maybe I'm too intense. Maybe I don't know the language. It's some key I don't have," she says, frustration edging into her voice. When she attends national workshops for her job as a television producer in St. Louis, she knows other people soon will be clicking and heading out for drinks at night. She admits she's not good at small talk, so often the lubricant to deeper connections.

She remembers having a few close chums in grammar school and high school, but she's never been able to recapture that as an adult. "My husband blames it on my not working hard enough at it. I thought it was more a matter of magic."

SOME SCARS DON'T HEAL

Unlike Rebecca, Betsy, a college professor on the East Coast, didn't even have close friends in grammar school. It was more like six bullies. Their teasing and exclusion echoes in her life to this day, tripping her up socially like a bad knee that never quite heals. "In fifth grade, I suddenly became the scapegoat. There were half a dozen of us who lived in the same direction from school. Suddenly they didn't want to walk with me. They made faces like I smelled bad and laughed and crossed the street to avoid me. It was out of the blue, organized by a girl I had particularly liked. It was devastating for me."

"I didn't play with them anymore, didn't go to movies, birthday parties, no hanging around on the playground, no jump rope. I had been a great rope swinger. Anytime they saw me, they would point and run away as if I were contaminated. I wanted to be invisible. I had no idea what had happened."

So Betsy, a bright, shy girl, escaped into the safer world of books. She read after school, on weekends, and during holidays. Terrified of being ostracized in high school, she became even more introverted. She eventually earned a Ph.D. and became a respected scholar in her field. But for all her academic achievement, she feels imperiled in ordinary social situations and crippled in the simple act of making friends.

It's hardest in a group. When Betsy walks into a PTA meeting or a party, her body tenses as if she were in physical danger, her heart crashing against her ribs. She's hypervigilant, her heightened radar set to detect any hint that she's not welcome. "I have a default setting that says, at best, I'm barely tolerated. I feel that if I do go up and make mindless small talk, that it won't work and people won't respond to me and suddenly I won't have any idea what to say."

She does wish she had more friends. "I'm lonely. I don't make friends that easily. I have difficulty picking up the phone and saying, 'Let's have lunch.' I have to work up my nerve. It takes unreasonable energy. I brood about it. If I do call somebody and they can't come or make a date and they break it, then I'm unlikely to try again."

Some shy women believe they are missing some elusive membership card that everyone else was issued at birth. They see a gap between themselves and women they perceive as smooth and confident. And there's the darker undertow, a tugging fear that somehow they're defective. These notions are all false.

STOP BEATING YOURSELF UP

Whenever a young Betsy hesitated before entering a party with a horde of cousins, her mother barked, "Don't be shy!" Finally, when Betsy was in her 40s, she announced to her mother, "You've never understood. I'm an introvert!"

Her mother slammed her fist on the table and shouted, "No,

you're not!" "It was as if I was coming out to her as a lesbian," re- calls Betsy wryly. Her critical mother may never accept it, but Betsy, the college professor, and Rebecca, the television pro- ducer, have learned to gently embrace their shyness. A funny thing happens when you start to like yourself; it's contagious.

"I'm trying to accept that part of myself and feel a little less anxious about it. I'm not judging myself as being less than other people," Rebecca says thoughtfully. "I used to project an un- comfortableness. Now I'm more relaxed and nicer to be around." In the past she was distracted by an internal voice that whispered insecurities when she met someone. "It said, 'What am I saying? Am I sounding stupid?' If you've not had the greatest track record, you can get obsessed thinking about 'Is this the point where I don't make friends? Is this where I give a bad impression?' It totally distracts you from being engaged in the conversation. Now, I'm listening and responding. I don't overcompensate and talk too much, which I sometimes found myself doing. And if there's no chemistry, I'm not criticizing my- self and that doesn't infect the next conversation I have."

Just a few weeks ago at a workshop, Rebecca saw a gleam of progress. She talked to more people and went out for burgers with a posse of colleagues. "I met a few people I'll stay in touch with," she says, sounding quietly pleased.

Rebecca recognizes that she makes friends slowly. "Maybe I'm a hard person to get to know quickly," she muses. "I come out in little bits, and that's okay."

As for Betsy, she sees her insecurity as that lame knee she has to coddle. When it flares up and taunts that nobody wants her around, she retorts, "That's old garbage. Stop thinking that!" When she's at a function and her tongue is glued to the roof of her mouth and she's so anxious it's hard to breathe, she tells her- self, "Close your eyes, take a deep breath. This is ridiculous!"

Her painful history, though, is not without its gifts. For one, she's more sensitive to others on the edges. She goes out of her way to smile at them, knowing how that relaxes her when she's feeling strange. And she's exquisitely thankful for friendship, a hungry woman who savors every kindness. "If somebody says, 'We missed you last week,' I'm always grateful. I'm always aware friendship is never to be taken for granted." She was still elated over an affectionate hug she'd received from a woman in her book group a week after it happened. "I replayed that scene about 16 times. She was really glad to see me," says a surprised Betsy.

Shy women may not realize that their reserve often is appreciated—a refreshing alternative to people who monopolize conversations and bulldoze anyone in their paths. When a friend was debating whom to invite to a new book group, she said, "I want quiet women. They make the most profound observations."

THE SIMPLE SECRET

If there's any secret to social success it's this: the people we like best are the ones who are interested in us. One of the most beloved men I ever met was my daughter's grammar school crossing guard, Vince. Vince was adored by everyone who drove or walked past his corner. A man in his 80s, he darted with the energy of a young sprout between cars waiting at the red light, just to say hi. "How are you?" he boomed into my window with a smile that seemed to harness the light of the sun. "I saw your husband on his walk this morning. Tell your daughter I'm giving away lollipops tomorrow!" Vince wasn't worried about whether I was happy to see him. He was just happy to see me and wanted to know how I was doing. I was crazy about Vince. He greeted just about every parent and kid by name. The sun shone brighter on his corner.

My family and I had breakfast one Saturday morning with

Vince. Over buttermilk pancakes drenched in maple syrup, he regaled us with stories of his various careers and charmed the curmudgeonly waitress, who gave us better service than usual. "What's his secret?" my husband and I asked each other after we'd said good-bye. We were both awed by Vince's aura. "He loves people," my husband finally said. It was that simple.

A Crisis Can Change Everything

Relationships are most comfortable when they click along at a predictable pace. You meet for lunch or a walk every few weeks. You call her, she calls you. You're fixtures in each other's lives. But when life pitches one of you a curveball, those rituals and rhythms may crumble. A person shifts into survival mode. The niceties of life—say, returning a phone call—strain one's capability. The friend in crisis will need support from you, though she has nothing to give at the moment. It's an unbalanced equation. Not everyone likes the math.

Some friendships weather the storm, others splinter on the rocks. Leslie Parrott, a marriage and family counselor and co-director for the Center for Relationship Development at Seattle Pacific University, saw both happen when she gave birth to a premature baby. Parrott had always invested a lot of energy in her pals. She met people for lattes in the morning before work, lunches between her classes, and book groups at night. Then Parrott's son was born at a frighteningly early six months.

"It was like I fell off the face of the earth," remembers Parrott. "I had a baby who was up 20 hours a day screaming and critically ill. He was tethered to a six-foot oxygen tank. I needed the most support I had ever needed in my life. I had these moments of awkwardness where people who I had dearly loved would come and it felt so much like they had no idea what was going on for me." A fissure appeared in relationships for the first time and steadily widened. "They didn't understand my inability to return a phone call. Friends would call and say, 'I've left you three or four messages and you haven't called me back.' For them it was so shocking that someone who had loved them for so long couldn't return their phone calls to say, 'I'm concerned about you; I need to know how you're doing.' It felt to them like I was shunning them. The truth was, it was beyond my capacity to return a phone call at that point. It showed me they had no feeling for my world."

It made Parrott reevaluate many relationships. "I realized some of my friends were wonderful as long as our lives were in sync. When our lives got out of sync, we weren't going to be able to hold on to it. It was sad, all those letting-gos."

Is it just selfishness when a person can't check her needs in the face of a friend's crisis? Perhaps the bigger culprit is insecurity. We rely on signals that our friends still love us—phone calls, making time to meet, hugs. When that reassuring flow is cut off, we panic, pout, and sometimes pull away. It's a disconnect that, without communication, can doom a relationship.

But some of Parrott's friends were confident and resourceful enough to stay in touch. "They said, 'Don't feel guilty if you can't call me back, but I might drop by.' They cared enough about me to keep trying. They didn't let me go."

One friend popped in unannounced and tossed her a new Bobbi Brown lipstick, ordering, "Put it on. You need it. You're still a woman!" Another delivered a giant exercise ball. "I heard on the radio if you bounce your baby on these balls they calm down," the friend said. "I felt so cared about when people would do that. I used that ball 15 hours a day for a while," Parrott recalls. And one pal picked her up at 6 A.M. to hit the drive-through latte stand, their babies strapped into car seats.

The friends that buttressed her in the first year of her son's life made a sacrifice, Parrott observed, because she couldn't reciprocate. It's more likely, however, that they considered it a privilege to help her. Who hasn't felt a flush of satisfaction after dropping off dinner to a sick pal or listening to her air a problem? And supporting a friend draws us closer to her. People often hold us at arm's length from their lives. But when they crack open the veneer of self-reliance, we all reap the pleasure of greater intimacy.

WHEN FRIENDS DISAPPOINT YOU

But what about those people who drop the ball in a crisis, the ones who disappear and disappoint? Do you jettison them because they didn't live up to your definition of *friend?* Suzy, who was diagnosed with ovarian cancer when she was 32, has softened towards the people who let her down. Initially, she crossed them off her list, mentally tracing an indelible black mark across the names of women who didn't call or visit. "I was hurt and confused," she says. "I remember thinking bitter thoughts about their deficiencies." But after time, she began to realize, "There are some people who can't handle it. I was so young and had lived a healthy lifestyle. A lot of people said, 'If it can happen to her, it can happen to me.' It scared them." On the other hand, some people she hadn't been close to wrote her compassionate notes and brought gifts and meals. "They were givers," she said. "In a crisis, they find a place for themselves."

Suzy realized a person's ability to hold her hand and negotiate the terrain of life-threatening illness was not a measure of the friend's affection. "People came up to me when I was out of the woods and my hair had grown back and apologized. They said they felt like they hadn't been a good friend." She witnessed her own limitations when one of her pals was hospitalized.

"When I went to the hospital to see him, I felt like I was going to pass out." She says that only now, having endured chemotherapy, does she "get" what a sick person needs: jokes, news about the world, care packages, dinner, no pity.

"Part of healing is not that someone has to apologize to you, but that you need to let go of why you're mad," says Tamara, a 38-year-old from suburban Chicago. She had been furious at people who withdrew from her when she learned her 2-year-old son had learning disabilities. Four years later, she's trying to release her anger. "I've learned not to judge people as friends because God only knows I've been judged. I can accept people and their limitations better." On the Jewish High Holidays, a traditional time of reconciliation, she called a couple she and her husband hadn't seen for years, even though they had once been inseparable. They met for dinner. "We spent three hours talking; we could have spent three more. They said they felt horrible because they don't know our children." Before they parted, the couple invited Tamara's family to their home for Hanukkah.

Will New Friends Ever Measure Up to Old?

"The idea of feeling vulnerable or intimate again with a new person is almost too much to bear. I don't want to go through all the breaking down of boundaries," confesses Sarah, a 42-year-old publishing executive in California. She recalls wonderful friends in New York, where she grew up, and other close pals when she moved to Denver. But when she packed up one more time to resettle with her husband and two children in L.A., the thought of starting over yet again was overwhelming. So she didn't.

"It's almost like you're competing with the past. I have a memory of what my friendships have been like and what they meant to me. I look around and think she [a new woman] doesn't measure up. I wonder, will anyone ever really understand me like my old friends did? I'm resistant to new friends because on some level, I can't believe I could ever be that close again to someone."

Some of Sarah's former best pals were members of Alcoholics Anonymous when she was becoming sober. It was a time when all artifice was stripped away. "On some levels, the healthier you become, the harder it is. We often bond at the site of our wounds," she says.

Now she settles for relationships of convenience. "They weren't chosen because our hearts connected. It's not that kind of deep connection that is really nurturing. We have some similar interests or we're thrown together because of work or geography. There is a sense of making do." But she also admits that she holds a piece of herself back, acknowledging, "If I met my new best friend, I don't even know if I'd recognize her."

Her resistance to taking a risk has left her emotionally isolated, since she had already let old friendships lapse. "Maybe I didn't return a phone call or write a letter or visit a friend," she says regretfully. She thought friendships—the time necessary to preserve old ones and nurture new ones—were for other people who weren't busy with demanding careers, a devoted family, or a beloved horse, which she rode every weekend. But then her mother became incapacitated and her family was thrown into turmoil. Heaped on top of that were disappointments at work. Sarah really needed a friend to confide in.

It's a conundrum. Sarah wants intimate connections, but she's hampered by the belief that no one can match her old friends. That attitude functions like one of those yellow wooden sawhorses that blocks a road. Heck, if many of us can land new and improved husbands after a divorce, it can't be impossible to find quality new friends. (And there are probably more good women out there than men!) Old friendships certainly have an irreplaceable richness and history. But the lens on memories is often smeared liberally with Vaseline, blurring the wrinkles. We tend to idealize old friends, which makes it harder for new ones to compete. And memories can't go out for sushi, or tell you if you look fabulous or dorky in those red suede desert boots, or drop off a bouquet of daisies when you're blue.

Taking a Risk: The Fear Factor

Something that also holds Sarah back from deeper friendships is the fear of exposing vulnerable parts of herself. She knows that's what it takes to create an intimate, authentic relationship. Old friends could catalog our flaws, but loved us anyway. A budding friendship has no such comfort zone. As one woman worried, "Will new people like my true self?"

It's a question we all ask. But for some it's especially hard to take that gamble. The reasons are varied and complex, but one may be our histories with parents and siblings. Those patterns can reverberate in our adult friendships, hampering or enhancing our ability to connect.

Judy Jordan, a clinical psychologist and researcher at the Stone Center, part of the Wellesley Centers for Women at Wellesley College in Massachusetts, explains that trust in relationships develops when a parent responds empathetically and lovingly to a child's emotions and needs. The child carries that trust—an unconscious blueprint of expectations—into adulthood. But if those needs are neglected, the child may have diminished expectations of relationships when she grows up. For her they've always been disappointing, hurtful, and confusing.

SARAH'S BABY STEPS

One day Sarah, the publishing executive, took a leap. She had long wanted to call a woman she saw at the horse stable on weekends to get together. "But I thought she was closer friends with the other women at the barn. I thought they might not want me," she explains, a common and often skewed perspective. She nervously dialed anyway. "I told her I didn't know why I hadn't reached out before, but I wanted to now and I'd like to spend more time with her and the others." It was at once a small and enormous step.

"To make the effort to get a friendship has a benefit in itself," Sarah discovered. "It was the act of doing something for myself that was important, whether or not it's successful." It was, though. The other women were welcoming and enthusiastic. "I felt like it broke down a little bit of the barriers between us. It's a process. It's not like when you were a kid. It will continue to take a conscious effort," Sarah observes. One she plans on making.

"Can I Trust Her?"

How do we gather the courage to unpeel the layers of our shiny social selves to our gritty core with a new person? By gradually learning whom we can trust.

"It's small steps," stresses Jordan, who also coauthored *Women's Growth in Connection*. "If you're trying to change a pattern of real disbelief in the responsiveness of others, you need to start with little things you try out, like, how did the person respond when I told them I was worried about my daughter? It's never jumping into blanket trust. It's tending to the emotional signals that the other person is present, responsive, and available."

Here are some questions to hone your instincts about whether a woman is worthy of your trust and friendship:

1. Do you feel like she's truly listening to you, or does she just want to talk about herself?
2. Can she accept your thoughts and feelings without judging or criticizing you?

3. Does she share information about herself, or is it one-sided? For a relationship to feel mutual, she needs to open up to you, too.

4. Does she gossip or spill other people's confidences or criticize them? If she does, then she'll probably do the same to you.

The Jealous Husband

Whenever Diane had a date to meet friends for dinner, her husband groused, "What are *we* supposed to do for dinner then? Why can't you see your friends during the daytime when I'm not around?" So she'd cook, feed her apparently helpless spouse and three kids, clean up the kitchen, and then go out. But even with the domestic front covered, she couldn't relax. "I always felt like I had to hurry up and get home. I'm looking at my watch thinking, 'Can I stay till 9:30? Will I get in trouble?'"

Trouble meant the silent treatment from her husband. If she got in "too late," he wouldn't talk to her. He punished Diane, a 48-year-old catering manager for a large hotel in Kansas City, for socializing without him.

Sound familiar? Although Diane's husband's response was extreme, many married women parry with resentful mates when they want to see friends. "If he comes home and I'm on the phone with a friend, he finds that particularly annoying," says Sheryl, 47, a life and career coach. "Like I'm supposed to be waiting at the door with my tail wagging, like the dogs. He'll roll his eyes at me and he'll say, 'On the phone *again*?' There's a real 'mommy pay attention to me!' element. It pisses me off."

Pissed or not, she and other women try to limit their calls to daytime hours to avoid a dustup. If a friend phones Sheryl in the

A Chat with Mr. Jealousy

So what's a woman to do when her partner frowns on her outings with pals? Here are some ideas to help you wave good-bye.

1. Explain to your husband why this time with friends is important to you. Tell him he'll benefit because it makes you a happier person.

2. Ask why he balks at your leaving. If he feels overwhelmed by cooking dinner for the family, hand him the phone number of a Thai restaurant that delivers and, if he's really flummoxed, write out the order. Or suggest places he can go for a casual bite, eliminating any dishes to wash (which might be left in the sink for you!).

3. Offer to alternate a weekly "guys' night out" with your "girls' night out."

4. Remind yourself that you deserve this date with pals. Take a lesson from Caroline, a newspaper reporter and mother of two, who reminds herself, "I'm entitled!"

5. Announce your plans; don't ask permission. Caroline says if her husband wants to grumble, that's his problem. She meets her posse once a month at a chic restaurant, orders sex on the beach (a neon tropical drink), and "takes a mental vacation."

evening for a nonurgent reason, she feels compelled to ask, "Can I call you back tomorrow?"

It doesn't take much to rev up our guilt machines, which are always idling in low gear anyway. A possessive spouse crimps our willingness to see or chat with pals in the evenings—sometimes the only time we have—and makes it harder to romp freely when we do. It's like going out with an anvil hanging from your neck.

What's behind their tantrums? Laziness, for one thing. They don't want to cook dinner, wrestle homework questions, and wrangle the kids into bed by themselves. Jealousy, for another. A man often views his wife as his best friend, sometimes his only friend. When she's gone or unavailable, he may feel lonely, angry, and even rejected.

"Men are big babies. They're really self-centered. They just think about themselves," says a 48-year-old male with a self-effacing grin. He, too, used to whine, "What am I supposed to do?" when his wife announced her plans to go out. But now, he says, "I've become more tolerant and accepting of my wife being with other people. It enriches her, it gives her different ideas, it's good for her networking. I realize it's good for me to get out and see friends, too. I've matured." He also realizes his wife's girlfriends take the pressure off his marriage. He can't meet all his wife's emotional needs, nor would he want to.

Here's a window into that experience for me. After my teenage daughter shot up to 5 feet 6 inches, she complained one night that her twin bed was too small. "I'll buy you a bigger one," I offered as I tucked her in.

"That's okay, I'll only be here for another three years," she informed me, already mentally packing her bags for college. I mournfully repeated the story to my husband. "Don't think about it," he said flatly. End of conversation.

The next day a friend with two sons in college offered a more sympathetic ear and made me laugh. "Don't worry, she'll keep coming back with her dirty laundry," she promised.

❦

The path to new friends is littered with roadblocks. We're too shy to try or we don't want to risk being vulnerable, even with someone who intrigues us. Obstacles may also trip up our existing friendships. But we can clear these hurdles like a high jumper who flies across the bar and lands in the soft sand. Like her, we need to muster our resolve and take a running leap—into a new relationship or away from a jealous husband, for a few hours, anyway.

PART TWO

The Tango of Friendship

10

Why You Need Pals

HOLLY and Eve pushed through the glass revolving door of their New York office building at 5:45 P.M. and clipped along Madison Avenue, immune to blaring horns and the jostling crowd. At the moment, Holly was venting about her bully of a boss. By the time they reached Grand Central Station, they were speculating whether their 16-year-old sons were having sex with their girlfriends. They veered to irritating habits of their husbands on the 32-minute train ride into New Rochelle.

When Holly's husband heard a car pull into the driveway, he peered through the kitchen window at Eve's silver Honda Accord. The two women were still engrossed in conversation, the motor running. As Holly finally stepped through the front door, he asked, genuinely mystified, "How can you still be talking? How can you still have more to say?"

"He doesn't get it," says Holly, 51, an executive for a national nonprofit agency in New York City.

But we do.

We have endless details to report to our friends, from the perfect red shoes we landed for half price at the Nordstrom's sale to the heart-thumping results of a breast biopsy. We have endless questions to ask them, calibrating their experiences against ours, searching for reassurance that we're doing okay. "Did your daughter think you were a hopeless moron when she turned 13?" a pal queries, relieved to know she is not the village idiot of mothers but part of the "village of idiot mothers," as experienced by all eighth grade girls. "Do you still sleep in the same bed as your husband?" another tentatively asks, happy to learn that she is not the only one who retreats to the guest bedroom when her mate's snores rattle the windows. Did your sister ever stop speaking to you? Does your mother still treat you like a child? If it's happened to our friends, too, we don't feel so alone and strange.

Boyfriends and husbands often can't provide the patient, empathetic ear we crave. When Holly relates some awful incident with her boss, her husband declares, "Why don't you tell her to go to hell?"

Thanks a lot, honey. "He doesn't understand there is complexity I have to deal with and need to talk about. He's not that sympathetic sometimes," she says. A man whips into his relationship toolbox—tiny as it is—and tries to fix a problem with a wrench twist of advice. Now, could you please hand him the remote and make some popcorn? "I don't need you to tell me what to do, I need you to listen," I've snapped at my poor husband numerous times. Many men, it seems, also have an abbreviated attention span for hearing your distress—limited to a commercial break or the blink of time between turning the sports pages of the morning newspaper.

But talking to another woman about a problem is like falling into a bed of pillows. We often find each other far more comforting than men when we're feeling stressed. In a study conducted by the University of California and Cornell University Medical College, men and women were asked to give impromptu speeches before an audience consisting of a supportive man or woman. The study found that a supportive female audience reduced cardiovascular stress responses for both the female and male speakers, while a supportive male audience did not. In a separate experiment in Germany, when women were asked to give a speech, their cortisol levels, a marker of stress, actually increased when they were with their boyfriends.

Females are hardwired to turn to other women in times of stress. It appears to be an ancient survival behavior that is deeply rooted in our biology and our genes. Hundreds of thousands of years ago, when women foraged for food and tended crops, they were less likely to end up as a lion's dinner or be attacked by males if they were in a group. Women who turned to their social group for help and protection were more likely to survive, as were their children.

Women's approach to coping with stress is different than men's, notes Shelley E. Taylor, a psychologist at UCLA who wrote *The Tending Instinct*. When faced with stress, men tend to either become aggressive or withdraw, which scientists call "fight or flight" behavior. A guy may brood on his La-Z-Boy. Women call a friend.

It's not surprising, then, that some women say they are more supported and understood by their friends than their husbands.

More than half the women responding to a 2002 *Ladies' Home Journal* survey said their best friends know them better.

R_x for a Long Life

The time we spend with close companions dramatically affects our happiness, our immune system, our cardiovascular health, our risk of developing a disease, how our bodies respond to stress, and the very length of our lives. It also appears to help protect us from depression. Social connections are not a luxury or an indulgence; they're essential to our well-being. Remember Holly's ride home from work with Eve? That socializing—as well as other visits Holly had with pals that week—enabled her to sleep more peacefully and may have helped her fight a cold. If she'd cut her finger, those visits might also have accelerated the healing.

"Women's friendships are vital to coping with stress, and how you cope with stress is vital to your life," Taylor says. In fact, she thinks a woman's means of coping—seeking out other women—may buffer her from stress's harmful effects and help explain why we live an average of six years longer than men.

Understanding exactly how companionship affects our physiology is a burgeoning, relatively new field. But one thing is already clear. People—both male and female—who have solid relationships with friends, family, and community live longer. Numerous studies done in the United States and other countries show that people who are isolated or disconnected from others have a two- to five-times-higher risk of dying. And while single, divorced, and widowed people have higher mortality rates than married ones, it's not the lack of a spouse that dooms them. It's the absence of a close pal or confidante, research shows.

The Friend Factor

Here's just a sampling of studies supporting the health benefits of friendship:

- One nine-year study showed that men who became widowed had an increased risk of dying. But the same wasn't true of women. The greatest effect on women's mortality was the number of contacts they had with close friends and relatives.

- When Dr. Redford Williams, director of the Behavioral Medicine Research Center at Duke University, studied more than 1,000 patients with coronary heart disease over five years, he and his team discovered, not surprisingly, that married patients survived longer than unmarried patients. But then they divided the unmarried patients into two categories—those with and without a close friend or confidante. Within those groups they found a dramatic difference. Half of the patients who were unmarried and did not have a confidante were dead within five years. About 85 percent of the unmarried patients with a confidante were still alive—the same survival rate as married individuals with a confidante.

- Stanford University psychiatrist David Spiegel discovered that group therapy for women with advanced breast cancer actually extended the women's lives. The women who attended a weekly support group, forming close bonds and offering each other emotional support after surgery, lived twice as long as those who didn't have the support.

A dearth of companionship even affects us when we lay our heads down on the pillow. John Cacioppo, a social neuroscientist and codirector of the Institute for Mind and Biology at the University of Chicago, found that both young and older adults who were lonely slept less soundly, waking more frequently and not accumulating as much deep sleep, than those who weren't lonely. His research also shows that their wounds didn't heal as quickly. And studies of isolated medical students showed yet another effect of isolation: they have lower levels of natural killer cell activity, which may diminish their ability to fend off illness.

"Human association is such a biological imperative, it is a need not unlike hunger. If people don't have social contacts, the biology doesn't function as well," said Cacioppo, who is heading a $7.5 million federal project to study how social isolation and loneliness affect health and the aging process.

HOW DO FRIENDS PROTECT US?

Scientists are just beginning to unravel the intricate mystery of the biological mechanisms that make friends powerful protectors of our health. But here's a look at how a visit or talk with a pal may diminish the harmful effects of stress on your body. Imagine you've just had an argument with your mother. As you slam down the phone, the stress hormones cortisol and adrenaline course through your system, signaling what they think is a life-and-death emergency. Your blood pressure surges as your heart begins pumping harder. Normally it pumps five quarts of blood per minute; now it's 20. This river floods your arteries and can damage and erode their lining, particularly with repeated stress.

The adrenaline also triggers fat to be released from fat cells into your bloodstream, providing energy to run for your life. But since you're just standing there fuming, the fat charges into your liver where it's converted to (primarily bad) cholesterol. This is the nasty stuff that ultimately turns into plaque, clogging your arteries and putting you at risk for a heart attack. Another unpleasant side effect of elevated cortisol is that it suppresses your immune system, which is why you are more susceptible to illness when you're under chronic stress. Cortisol can decrease the number of infection-fighting cells and depress their ability to ward off disease.

But say, instead of stewing, you pick up the phone and call Betsy. She listens sympathetically and, perhaps, offers a bit of wisdom or a fresh perspective. As you talk, your shoulders un-clench from around your ears and the hammer stops pounding on your left temple. Your body recalls its emergency messengers as your heart rate slows and cortisol levels recede to normal. It's chronic stress—say, ongoing hostility with your mother or boss or spouse—rather than occasional bursts of it that ravages your health. Having a trusted friend mitigates the damage.

In fact, just knowing you have a social lifeboat—what scientists call perceived support—guards your health. In one study, people who believed a helpful person was available to them when they gave a public speech—purely an illusion of support since the person didn't actually exist—had lower blood pressure before and during the speech than those who didn't think they had help.

The Happiness Factor

We may not be aware of friendship's dramatic impact on our physiology, but we sure know how it buoys our mood. A rowdy Wednesday night book group lights up our circuits like a power surge. After I chat with Caroline, my lively, funny friend in Washington, D.C., I'm recharged, even if I felt like a slug when I first picked up the phone.

Conversely, who hasn't started to feel gloomy and feckless after spending too many hours—not by choice—by herself? Certainly, we all have different social appetites, but long stretches of isolation drag many of us down.

Just how strongly do friends influence our emotional states? The more close friends women have, the more they describe themselves as "very happy," according to a 1998 survey from the National Opinion Research Center at the University of Chicago.

And the more friends you collect from different parts of your life, the less likely you are to catch a cold. Sheldon Cohen, a psychology professor at Carnegie Mellon University in Pittsburgh, exposed people to a virus that causes a common cold. Who started sneezing? The ones with fewer relationships. It wasn't just having a bunch of friends that protected them but the diversity of those connections, such as family, close neighbors, friends, colleagues, or members of a religious or volunteer group. Cohen thinks it makes a lot of sense. "You see yourself as being this complex person. It reduces general anxiety and makes you less susceptible to things that happen in different roles in your life," he says.

Ultimately, though, it's the quality of relationships, not the sheer number of them, that infuses your life with pleasure and health perks. These are the friends who spark your energy, care about you as much as you care about them, and fan your dreams.

Why Friends Buffer Our Moods

How do good friends yank the clouds on our moods? It's a simple but powerful reason: they remind us we are not alone. "One of the places for real suffering for human beings is the feeling of isolation: When a friend nods her head or says, 'I've been there' or 'I know what you mean,' you know you're not the only one who's been through this. You don't have to be ashamed," says Judy Jordan, a clinical psychologist, author, and researcher in women's relationships at the Stone Center, part of the Wellesley Centers for Women at Wellesley College in Massachusetts.

When I was bereft over a looming change in my life, Carol listened sympathetically while we slurped chicken-noodle soup at a coffee shop, and declared, "Of course, you're upset. This is traumatic stuff." That made me feel enormously better. I wasn't a wimp, at least not about this, and it didn't hurt that she handed me a comfort bag of new chocolate-cream Oreos. Carol and I, confirmed chocoholics, give chocolate to celebrate or soothe.

Friends are neon orange life preservers when the sea is churning around us. When Sandy's 8-year-old daughter was diagnosed with leukemia, she was swept into an alien universe of chemotherapy treatments, surgeries, and lengthy hospital stays. Her life as she had known it disappeared. For six months friends ferried roast chicken and spaghetti dinners to Sandy's family—dropping the food off in a special cooler outside the back door of her house. Her husband toted the meals to the hospital room so they could all eat a hot, homemade dinner together—a soothing break in their raw days. Still, Sandy rarely saw her loving friends.

But women don't want to endure a crisis alone. Sandy and the other mothers on the pediatric oncology floor forged new friendships within a matter of weeks. "They became my new neighborhood," she recalls. "We ended up recreating the community of friends we had in our normal life." In fact, this was the very community she needed, women who were enduring the same surreal existence that she was. Like her, they slept each night on hard leather chairs next to their children's hospital beds, could analyze white blood cell counts with the expertise of an oncologist, tucked away their terror every morning to face their children. Sandy no longer felt adrift as she and the other moms swapped medical tips, chortled at each other's black humor, and helped the intolerable become less so.

Leslie Parrott, a marriage and family therapist, recalls her spiraling mood when she was restricted to bed rest during her second pregnancy. "My husband couldn't bear the burden of every depressing thought I had. He just couldn't do it. If I start talking that way my husband's face clouds over. I see him thinking, 'How will we cope?'" says Parrott. But her friends perched on her bedside and listened without cloudy faces. "They weren't threatened by the depth of my emotions. It didn't rock their world." After their visits, Parrott's heaviness lifted. But she wasn't the only one reaping benefits. Her friends did, too. Providing support makes you feel like an integral part of another person's life and that you matter.

But pals don't have to cook us dinner or listen to our problems for us to appreciate them. In fact, research shows that the simple pleasures of companionship—seeing the latest chick flick together or riding your bikes to Dairy Queen for a hot fudge sundae—are the most satisfying part of friendship and the most critical in staving off loneliness.

YOU CAN HAVE TOO MANY FRIENDS

There's no magic number of friends. For some women, there's even a downside to a bounty of pals. The demands of those relationships loom like another "to-do list" in their already frantic lives.

"Friendships are a mixed blessing," sighs Jackie, 46, who is in frequent touch with a dozen pals, many of them from college. "I worry, am I being a good enough friend? This one's dad had surgery, did I remember to call? Whose birthday was it? My friends helped me through a lot of tough periods. I wonder, am I doing the same in return? The obligation of a friendship weighs heavily on me. I don't think I do a very good job of it."

If Jackie's not doing a good job, heaven help the rest of us. Here's a sampling of what she did for them one recent week: drove Amy's daughter to school events because Amy was out of town, spent 10 hours on various days packing boxes for a newly divorced neighbor who was moving, scoured shops with Joy to help her pick a dress for her daughter's bat mitzvah, met Shelly at a furniture store to choose a lamp for her house (Jackie's friends think she has great taste). In between racing around for her buddies, Jackie runs a fashion accessories business, has three children, a husband, and a seriously ill father.

It is possible to overdose on socializing. "The phone is always ringing," Jackie complains. "I feel like I cannot have one train of thought all the way through without being interrupted." She's not kidding. During my 30-minute phone conversation with her, call waiting beeped. "Sorry, I'll be right back," she said, then jumped back on, reporting, "It was a friend." A few minutes later, it beeped again. "Just a second," she said, sounding harried. Another friend had called.

The Wrong Friends Are like a Bad Virus

Friendship can heap extra stress on your life if a relationship sours. Research by Janice Kiecolt-Glaser, a professor of psychiatry at The Ohio State University, shows that hostile arguments between husbands and wives weaken women's immune responses and hike their stress hormones. Interestingly, men's hormone levels do not change after an argument. The reason, researchers believe, is women are more sensitive to negative behaviors in their relationships. It's not too much of a leap to imagine that acrimony or a fight in an intimate friendship could deal a similar blow to a woman's health. (In fact, another study showed that negative social ties have a greater impact on a woman's well-being than positive ones.)

That was Samantha's experience. An unraveling relationship with a woman she thought was her best friend unleashed a wave of physical ailments. Samantha and Anna were so close that when Anna was pregnant with her third child, she asked Samantha to shop for all the baby's clothes because she was too exhausted. Knowing her pal's discriminating taste, Samantha spent days in stores all over her Long Island suburb choosing the outfits she thought Anna would love. She even loaned her a bassinet.

Then Anna met one of Samantha's neighbors at a dinner party at Samantha's house. The neighbor, a notorious gossip and social climber, glommed on to Anna. The neighbor, Karen, connived to become friends with her. She also tried to poison Anna and Samantha's friendship by fabricating nasty stories about Samantha. Anna started doing more and more with Karen and excluding Samantha. The coup de grace was when Anna and her husband were driving with Samantha and her spouse to a restaurant for dinner. Anna blithely announced that she was canceling their long-standing plans to take a Utah ski vacation together. "Samantha, you're going to totally freak out," Anna said, "but we're going with Steve and Karen because they have a private jet."

"I felt like I'd been stabbed," recalls Samantha. "I thought, 'Oh, I get it. If I had a private jet, you'd go with me.' I didn't know what to believe about us as friends anymore."

By the time they arrived at the bistro, Samantha was practically blinded by an aura of flashing lights in her eyes, a prelude to her migraine. When the headache struck, she was in such pain, she excused herself from the table and took a cab home. The next day, gossip rippled through the tony suburb about Samantha's "hissy fit" in the restaurant because Anna wouldn't go on a ski trip with her. The rumor could only have been started by Anna.

When she grasped the global betrayal of her friend, "It made me sick to my stomach," says Samantha. "It was like I broke up with my boyfriend." She lost her appetite and was nauseous for months. The stress kicked up her acid reflux, producing a burning sensation in her esophagus. She also was wracked by a series of migraines and sinus infections. Being wounded by and losing a once-dear friend roiled her health. Several years later, she's reluctant to make new friends, skittish about whom she can trust.

Take a Leap!

But even when the occasional bad friendship knocks us down in the dirt, we need to dust ourselves off and try again with someone new. The perks of caring pals are too good to miss. Friends nudge and inspire us to take a leap that we might never have braved on our own. When I was a feature writer for the *Chicago Sun-Times* in the mid-1980s, my friend Betsy, a reporter for another newspaper, called to announce she was flying to Washington, D.C., to cover the late Princess Diana's first official trip to the United States. "Ask to go!" she prodded. Betsy always charged confidently into the thick of news stories. "I . . . I don't know," I stammered, a swarm of moths fluttering wildly in my stomach. Big stories scared me. I worried that I would blow it. "You can do it," she cajoled. Thanks to her, I covered Princess Diana's arrival. The highlight was a royal cocktail party where I frantically tried to perfect my curtsy in the receiving line before I greeted the royal couple. I chatted a bit with the loquacious Prince Charles. The princess reminded me of a shy giraffe.

Several decades later, Carol kicked me in the butt to get moving on this book. She had patiently listened to me wax for years about the book I wanted to write "when I was ready." "You know, you're not going to live forever," she commented bluntly one day. She was right. It was the push I needed.

Gazing into a Kinder Mirror

Intimates often reflect back a gentler vision of ourselves than the one we see. I often beat myself up about my imperfections as a mother, which glare at me in a giant, magnifying mirror. Last summer, I fretted to a friend because I was working every day and not ferrying my daughter to the beach and the pool. My friend pointed out that I was setting an example of a mom that could grant herself time away from her family to pursue a passion. My guilt ebbed . . . well, mostly.

Friends assuage our guilt, ease our stress, make us laugh, recharge our energy, carry our grief, and celebrate our successes. Now scientists are discovering that this emotional jackpot—like lining up triple sevens on a Vegas slot machine—pays off like a gush of shiny quarters in terms of our health. People with trusted confidantes have feistier immune systems and healthier cardiovascular systems. And as a result, they live longer—all thanks to their friends.

But we don't think about science and longevity when we're sipping a glass of wine with a pal in an outdoor cafe on a soft summer night. We just know we're having fun and don't want to go home.

We're more attractive, witty, and kind in the refracted gaze of our buddies. Pals see us through a rosier lens than spouses, boyfriends, and children. My husband, whom I adore, nevertheless some nights views me primarily as a woman with cluttered countertops, stacks of uncashed paychecks, and overflowing laundry baskets. My teenage daughter is mortified by everything I say, wear, or do. Enter a friend whose voice lifts in pleasure when she hears me on the other end of the line. "It's so good to talk to you," a long-distance pal enthused the other morning. Suddenly, I'm worthwhile again.

11

Learning the Delicate Dance

○═══╋═══○

IT'S EASY to get your feet tangled in the tango of friendship. There are enough missteps and miscues that even the most practiced partners can lose their rhythm. New partners have it even rougher as they try to intuit each other's mysterious dips and turns for the first time. Understanding the intricate steps can determine the fate of a fresh or even a seasoned relationship. Some of us sway to a different beat and that trips us up.

We read friendship between the lines. Silences thunder: the unreturned phone call, the unreciprocated invitation. Often, we misinterpret.

We can attempt to demystify the dance. Why do some of us want to gab once a week, while others feel smothered by that pace? Why doesn't a friend return phone calls? How do you shake off bruised feelings? What's the right pace for a blossoming friendship? How do you parry a rebuff? When should you give up?

The answers, hopefully, will keep you on the dance floor.

The Confusing First Steps

Almost any woman who's tried to make a new pal in midlife suddenly feels like she's standing on the dance floor with two left feet. We should know this tango by heart—after all, we made friends easily enough when we were younger. But now we can't quite recall the rhythm or the steps. Shortly after I moved here, I initiated a couple of lunch dates with a woman I liked. Then I waited. It was her turn to call now, wasn't it? But she didn't. I stewed and waffled over what to do. Would I seem pushy if I called again? Was she trying to tell me something? Why is this so damn hard?

A lot of reasons. When you're a high school or college student or even a neophyte in a career, your dance card is open. Whether you've just unpacked your suitcase in the freshman dorm or landed in your first law firm job, you're hungry to meet people. Act I of Momentous Life Events pitches us toward each other with a powerful force. We want to thrash over confusing new experiences and anxiously compare notes. We're all at the same stage. Friendships gel as we map new terrain together and build a history. Connections are as malleable as wet clay, and groups are still coalescing amidst big batches of time to just hang out.

But just a decade or so after career start-ups, many people sport a flashing neon NO VACANCY sign above their heads. They've traipsed past those "bonding firsts." There is less that draws them naturally to new people. Relationships have solidified, sometimes ossified. If you jump to a new office when you're 40, you may be eating lunch alone at your desk—as my friend Caroline discovered when she joined a prestigious East Coast newspaper. The reporters were cordial but indifferent, a radical change from the friendly southern daily paper she worked at in her late twenties. There, she and the other women threw each other baby showers and invited each other's families over for dinner.

Snaring a new friend now often requires a Herculean effort, Teflon-glazed feelings, and the persistence of Sisyphus.

Dance Lessons

New relationships require finesse. If you're overzealous, you may scare someone away. Likewise, detaching too early—an "if she doesn't call me this time, I'm not calling her again" attitude—may pinch a bud before it blooms. We used to plot like this to lure a boyfriend or a mate. Now it's friends.

So, would it have been okay for me to call my new pal one more time? Yes, but not too soon. The primal rule is don't look desperate, even if you are very desperate indeed. "It's a turnoff," author Martha Bullen says bluntly. She has several cross-country moves under her belt. "People will be worried about getting involved with you. They think you may be clingy, that you'll be at their doorstep every day." Bullen watched a new friend of her daughter's follow her around all day at school. "It drove her crazy. I thought, this is not a good way to start. You have to play it more cool. Not like, 'If you don't become my friend, I'll go jump off a bridge.' You can go into a deep depression going through these life changes," she acknowledges, "but you don't want to convey that you are teetering on the edge."

That's easy to say when a friendly face looks like the only lifeboat in sight. But save your tale of loneliness for the friends you left behind or a newcomers' group where other women are treading the same water. It's tempting to unload on the first kind person you see, assuming if she knows how unhappy you are, she'll sign up to be your friend. She won't. People are attracted to you because of your delightful personality, not because they feel sorry for you.

When you're trying to snare a new pal, it's reasonable to initiate three get-togethers. After that, though, if the other person doesn't reciprocate, it's time to reassess. Does she work full time, have kids and a horde of friends? She'll be less available than a woman who has fewer ties and demands on her time. While she may enjoy your company, you'll need to take a number to see her. Temperament is another factor. Some women crave daily contact with friends; others need more space.

You can't force a relationship to take root, no matter how much you cultivate it. That's what a transplanted Oklahoma City woman reluctantly accepted after she initiated six dates with a woman in her suburb west of Chicago. "I thought, if I keep making the effort, this friendship will really become important to both of us. My family said, 'Give up!'" She finally did.

An Awkward Conversation

If you sense a mutual fondness, it's worth gently addressing the issue before you call it quits. Judy Jordan, a clinical psychologist, suggests saying, "'I've noticed that I'm the one who is always calling to get together. I need to check out with you if I am looking for more time together than you really would like or do we have a style difference here?' That way you're not putting her on the spot and saying, 'I'm mad that you haven't called me.'" You may not always get an honest answer, but it's worth a try. She may say she likes being with you, but it's too much for her to meet once a week. Maybe she prefers once a month. If you can accept her rhythm, you can preserve the connection. "If you don't have that conversation, you run the risk of losing the relationship altogether," says Jordan.

Even older relationships are rarely perfectly balanced. One woman often assumes more responsibility for a friendship, checking in more often and planning the dates. Bullen is the executive director of many of her friendships, a role she now accepts fairly gracefully. "I used to feel a little hurt and think, 'Why do I always have to be the one to call?' The more I thought about it, I realized it was a personality difference. They say, 'Oh yeah, I was thinking of giving you a call,' but then they go on to the next thing. When I call they say, 'Great, let's get together.' Plus, I've trained them. They know I'm going to call and e-mail them at some point. I put in a lot of effort."

But most of us want some reciprocity. Fifty-fifty isn't necessary, but at least 70-30; okay, even 80-20. It's a particularly touchy issue in the dawn of a relationship. My stomach was clutching as I sat across the table from Sharon, a dear new friend. Whenever I phoned she said, "I've been thinking about you!" But I always made the call to meet, and after six months it had begun to make me uncomfortable. So now I nervously told her. She put down her turkey sandwich, listened thoughtfully, then admitted, "I'm not good at calling." It wasn't her lack of affection; it was personal style. We resolved that by setting up monthly lunches, eliminating the issue of whose turn it is. We also look for classes to take together. Our most recent: pet telepathy. No kidding.

Without that awkward conversation, a relationship can fracture. Indeed, I sidestepped that pothole with one friend for years. She was busier than me — so I told myself it was okay that I always called her. But eventually, it began to chafe. I finally stopped calling, and she slipped into the watery undertow of lost friends. A discussion wouldn't have changed her, but it might have cleared the air enough for us to work out an arrangement that didn't feel so one-sided. And hearing her side of it might have helped me understand how she viewed us and recalibrate my expectations. My cowardice ultimately doomed the friendship. Ironically, she didn't even notice my withdrawal. I bumped into her a year later in a store and was wrapped in a big hug. "Let's get some coffee," she said. We caught up, but for me it wasn't the same. My heart was shuttered.

You're Hungry, She's Not

People have wildly varying social appetites. Some are voracious eaters, heaping their plates with huge portions from a giant buffet of pals. Others are nibblers, easily sated with a bite here and there. Understanding those differences may illuminate — and depersonalize — why some women rarely pick up the phone or embrace an overture of friendship.

The personalities of extroverts and introverts offer a window into these varying styles. Extroverts thrive on lots of interactions. Introverts are drained by too much time with people. They need fewer friends and less time with them. "They're picky eaters," explains Janet Penley, whose Chicago-area consulting business helps women understand how they interact with the world through a personality questionnaire, women's circles, and workshops.

An introvert herself, Penley admits, "It's always biting me in the butt. I try to keep up with the extroverts, but I can't. There are a lot of women out there who are interesting to me, but I just don't have the energy to maintain a lot of friendships. As frustrating as it is, I know I have a limit on how big my social circle can be. I'm happier with fewer friends." For Penley, a "crammed" social calendar consists of a once weekly yoga and Spanish class, plus "maybe I can handle a lunch with a friend once a week." Usually she and her husband (another introvert) hang out by themselves on weekends.

Dueling social needs can challenge friendships between an extrovert and an introvert. Penley had one close friend who called too often for her taste. "I didn't want to spend that much time with her," she says. So she invented excuses or sometimes went along even if she didn't want to. The friend picked up on Penley's ambivalence and confronted her. Penley explained that they were out of sync and arranged a less intense schedule. The friendship survived.

But not all do. "I really need my personal space," explains Nadia, 43, an at-home mom in suburban Kansas City. "I've lost some friends because they're the lunch-bunch type and I'm not. I don't answer the phone all the time. I'm not a person who is going to blab with you every day." She may not return a phone call for several weeks; sometimes never. Like Penley, she prefers having only a few friends and doesn't feel the need to keep in frequent touch.

One of Nadia's friendships recently flamed out over her desire for alone time. "You never make time for us!" the woman griped. "I can't live up to your expectations," Nadia responded. Another pal, Dina, downgraded Nadia to her B-list of buddies after being frustrated by her for years. "I've told her that it bothers me that she can't call me back and she doesn't keep up with the friendship," Dina says. "I have accepted it, but she's not on par with other friends I have. We might go a for a long time without talking."

If you want to keep a friend like Nadia, remember that her inability to call is a limitation of *hers*. "She may not be able to do this, even though she cares about you a lot. It involves a certain empathy with the other person," says Jordan. A way to cope with these limits is to focus on making your other relationships more evenly balanced.

When a Friend Loses Touch

Empathy is also helpful when a friend suddenly neglects the relationship or falls out of touch for no discernable reason. You may be tucked in her heart, but not in her immediate consciousness, when she's busy or distracted. That's what I reminded myself about my long-distance buddy, Caroline.

She and I e-mail each other nearly every weekday—sometimes twice a day—epistles that leap from which style gray pants she should order from Eddie Bauer online (flat front, wool, I advised after browsing the Web site) to ruminations about a spouse's crankiness.

So when I zipped her a couple missives and didn't hear back right away, I chalked it up to a busy week. More time passed. Maybe she didn't get the e-mails, I mused. A few more days and my thoughts darkened. Maybe I've done something to offend her. The following week, when I still hadn't heard from her, I brooded that I obviously wasn't as important to her as she was to me.

Is this ridiculous? Of course. Embarrassing? Yes. Am I the only one who obsesses over unreturned e-mails and phone calls? I doubt it. There are plenty of times I would have just written her again and not fretted over it. But perhaps I was feeling sensitive that week. Eventually, I e-mailed her again and we resumed our routine. I didn't bring up the long stretch of silence at the time, though I have to admit, it smarted for a while. Ultimately, though, I kept sight of the bigger picture—a long and lovely friendship—and moved beyond my nicked ego.

(P.S. I nervously read her this section while I was writing the book, and she didn't recall a thing about being incommunicado. "Gosh, I'm sorry," she said. "I must have been distracted." Keep that in mind the next time you take a friend's silence personally.)

Many of us personalize and imagine slights where none are intended. Next time I'll try relationship guru Harriet Lerner's suggested strategy: a lighthearted and non-guilt-inducing, "Have you been really busy or have my e-mails been lost in space?" One of my friends has an excellent way of signaling she's too busy to communicate: "Am crazed. Real e-mail later," she writes.

The Alchemy of Attraction

Some people have chemistry, some don't. A woman's hairstyle, the lilt of her voice, her clothes, her sense of humor, her attitudes all blend in an elusive alchemy that either enchants us or leaves us cold. That attraction is so powerful, some women describe the moment they met as "love at first sight."

Because most women are pickier as they get older, it becomes harder to find someone who wows us. After one woman took a "social test drive" with some people she'd met, she lamented, "This one's too bossy, that one's too boring." Our time is precious and we don't want to waste it.

That said, you're not always whacked by a lightning bolt the first time you meet someone. It may be a slow dawning of, "Hey, I really like this person." That's how it was with my former next-door neighbor. I first met Lily when she corralled my husband and me in the driveway as we toured our new house. Her hair was wild and uncombed, pants and shirt rumpled. "Got any kids? Got any animals?" she interrogated me with a piercing stare. Let me just say, Lily didn't appear to be fertile friend material. But when our moving van pulled up one icy January morning, she dashed out with a pot of coffee and her best bone china cups on a silver tray. When I became pregnant, she was the one I trusted to be my backup childbirth partner in case my husband was caught out of town. And after I had the baby, my phone would often ring at 7 P.M. with her generous offers of leftovers. "Want some stir-fried beef? We figured you probably hadn't eaten." She was right; I hadn't. Lily, who was earning her Ph.D. in psychology, became a good friend. It just took me a while to excavate the brilliant emerald beneath her rugged exterior.

"I WANT TO BE LIKE YOU"

We are often drawn to a woman who dazzles us—by her self-assuredness, career success, or panache with clothes. "We would like to think of ourselves as similar to her in certain ways, but maybe we don't feel we get there ourselves," explains Luise Eichenbaum, a psychologist and coauthor of *Between Women: Love, Envy, and Competition in Women's Friendships*. The traits we admire are clues for changes we desire in ourselves. Connecting with a woman we admire makes it easier for us to be like her.

The qualities that attract us may shift radically throughout our lives. "In my thirties, I looked for women who were company. My friends had kids of a similar age as mine and were in a similar place," says Nashville publisher Amy Lynch. She was ghostwriting books and freelancing articles, but her primary focus was her family.

When her kids became teenagers and Lynch hit her mid-forties, however, her attention pivoted. She had long heard a quietly persistent inner voice wondering, "Could I publish more meaningful books? Could I start a publishing house?"

Suddenly the women with whom she had spent lingering

lunches and long hours shopping felt peripheral to her life. They were still tracing the same familiar path while Lynch had veered off to scale a brambly, unmarked trail. Now she sought women who embodied the talents she wanted to spawn in herself. She drew close to a sometime–jogging partner, a single woman, ambitious and assertive, who ran her own business. "When I started talking about the struggle to be something more, this friend would look at me and nod in a way that let me know she had been there. She clearly understood that hunger in me. The other thing she does for me is say, 'I believe in you. You've never spoken before 700 people before, but of course you can do it.' Those are the greatest words you can hear from a friend."

Lynch soon launched and became the editor of an award-winning newsletter for parents called "Daughters." Then, in 2003 she created "Ourselves," a newsletter for women about the emotional and spiritual changes in midlife. Lynch's new friendships flung open a door to a part of herself she had only dreamed about and helped propel her to new successes.

SEEKING A DOUBLE

Some women seek a twin in a friend, choosing women with mirror backgrounds, likes, and dislikes. Maura discovered that when she struck up a conversation with Jane at the Massachusetts health care company where they worked. "You look familiar," Jane had said. "Funny, you do, too," Maura had replied.

"There was something about her that I recognized," explains Maura, although they'd never actually met before. They soon unpeeled layer upon layer of astonishing similarities. "We were brought up Irish Catholic. We both like antiques, nice dishes, nice linens, and we like to cook good food and have parties." When they shop at antique stores, they pick up the same bowls to admire, thinking of all the generations of cakes that have been mixed in them. And they even agree that Brigham's chocolate chip ice cream is the world's best.

"It's a recognition that you were absolutely meant to be friends," says Maura. What adds sweetness to the relationship is their age difference: Maura is 37, Jane 53. When they're out together, they get asked whether they're mother and daughter, which pleases them. "My mother was my best friend," says Maura, whose mom has Alzheimer's.

An Unhealthy Attraction

But sometimes the qualities that lure us reflect a darker, unhealed dimension. For a long time, Stella, a 48-year-old novelist and screenwriter in Berkeley, California, was entangled with narcissistic women. "They were people like my mother. They could only look at the world from their point of view, who acted as if the whole world revolved around them. People were coming to me in a crisis all the time and expecting me to rescue them. But if I needed to depend on them for anything, they weren't there."

"I kept looking for women friends where I could re-create my relationship with my mother and have it work out better. It didn't work out better. It worked out the same."

One prime example was a new woman with whom Stella felt "a spark of friendship." The woman asked to borrow her sewing machine. Even though it was pouring out, Stella drove it over. "I had a flat tire when I got there and asked if she could help me fix it. She said, 'I have to take a nap.' I wound up fixing the flat tire all by myself in the rain. She was somebody whom I was very attracted to as a friend. It typified that kind of thing."

When Stella recognized the pattern, she severed the lopsided friendships and sought new ones. "It was like a vacuum.

All these emotionally nurturing friends rushed in. They were much healthier relationships." When she jettisoned the selfish pals, she had the energy and time to seek out more giving ones.

In the Beginning, Zip Your Lip

Two women feel a mutual sizzle of interest in each other. Will the relationship soar or belly flop? Some of that depends on how much they reveal about themselves and when. Too much too soon crushes a fledgling relationship, like an avalanche on a fragile frame.

Judy Jordan suggests saving seriously private information until you've constructed a solid foundation. "As much as we may feel an initial rush of trust when we meet somebody new, a sense that this person is going to be my friend, a feeling of warmth and hope, people need to remember that relationships are built gradually. That means not rushing in with your whole life story. Err on the side of being a little more cautious. There will be time to reveal the more vulnerable part of yourself in the future," she says.

When I lived in Dallas, I casually knew a lively woman I liked. I suggested we take a bike ride one morning. The first time we had ever said more than 'Hi, howareyou?' she revealed the details of every significant problem in her life—her physically abusive husband, ensuing divorce, and a wrenching childhood. By the end of the hour, I was reeling. "I'm so sorry," was all I could say, over and over. There was no gradual unfolding, no sense of emerging discovery—one of the joys of a new friendship. I always kept her story in confidence, but wondered if she regretted divulging so much before she really knew me. I suspected this because when I bumped into her after that, her once warm greetings had become chilly. We never got together again.

What else was wrong with this picture? She learned nothing about me that day. I was merely a witness to her pain.

Parrying a Rebuff

Rejection stings like sunscreen in your eyes. But it's rarely because of anything you did wrong. It's almost always about the other person—her limited time (she has enough friends) or her needing something you don't have, no matter how charming you are.

For instance, one woman in her early 50s is courting only "vibrant, stylish, older women" as new pals "because that's who I want to become. I'm looking for models," she says. Another one is drawn to trendy dressers because she wants help in that area.

You get the point. The more you remind yourself of people's differing needs, the more quickly you'll recover. Soon, rebuffs will feel more like a paper cut than a stab wound.

I was given the brush-off by a teaching assistant at my daughter's school. We got together once and had a good time. At least, I did. A few weeks later, I saw her sitting at a table by herself in a bakery. As I walked up to say hello, she thrust her hand protectively over the space next to her and blurted, "I'm waiting for someone!" She might as well have shoved me. Perhaps because I'm slow, or couldn't quite fathom why she was so unfriendly, I popped into her classroom one day—after hours—when I happened to be passing by. She never looked up from her task as I greeted her. I got the hint. Sure, I was bruised, but I didn't obsess over it.

"Before, if someone didn't like me or we didn't become friends, I would have wondered if I did something wrong," muses Lynch, the publisher. "I take all that less personally than

Rallying after a Rejection

Consider these your rejection mantras. Repeat them to yourself if you get the cold shoulder. They really help.

1. I'm a good person, and I deserve great friends.
2. It's not about me. She already has enough friends and doesn't have room for anyone else.
3. Maybe she doesn't think we're a good match. I'll eventually find someone who does. Not everybody can love me.
4. She may be depressed or going through a crisis.
5. Perhaps my personal situation threatens her in some way.

I used to." When dinner conversation with a prospective new friend fell flat, she says, "I walked away and thought, 'Well, okay, we're not in the same place.' You take it more in stride. It's very powerful for me to be able to do that. It makes me think about how I grew up, wanting to please everybody. That's profound change."

If rejection is a long-term pattern, though, you may want to join a therapist-led support group for insight into why nobody accepts your overtures of friendship. Maybe you are coming on too strong and scaring people away or making some other "mistake." Professional guidance might help. (Turn to the next chapter on friendship busters and boosters for advice about behaviors that enhance or erode relationships.)

When the Music Stops

Every friendship has a natural life span. I have one that's thrived for more than forty years. I met Susan in preschool, where her first memory is of me biting her on the arm. Luckily, she doesn't hold a grudge. We survived living together in college, question-able boyfriends, a divorce, and miscarriages. We've fought (she threw her Barbie doll at me in second grade) and always made up. I admit when I let her down, and when she disappoints me, I tell her. Mostly we prop each other up. Our friendship will endure as long as we do.

Another relationship flickered out in about a year, its wick necessarily shorter. This woman and I met peeling off our sweaters on the steamy bench of our kids' winter swimming lessons. We were both lonely then and connected around that. Every week after swimming, we hit a cheap pizza place with our kids and talked. When the lessons ended, we only stayed in touch for a few months. We'd each moved on. It was a natural end to a relationship that had served our needs. They're not all meant to last forever.

But endings can be thorny when one person has let go and the other hasn't. A pal of Janet Penley's suddenly became too busy to see her. "She's chosen other people to get closer to than me," says Penley. "I thought, 'Why does she like somebody more than me?' Maybe the chemistry isn't there. It hurts a little bit because you think everyone should think you're wonderful. But it's not earth-shattering."

Penley is philosophical about endings. "I don't hold on to the relationship if the other person senses it's time to move on. I honor that. I'm always moving on to meet my changing needs. Why shouldn't she?" She is attuned to the signals of the passive good-bye. "Maybe you invite them to do something and they can't and you don't feel a lot of energy to create an alternative date. You have less and less in common when you get together."

So she loosens the mooring. But that undiscussed drifting can leave a key question hanging: is the relationship dead or merely dormant? When Penley drove past her old friend's house the other day she felt a brush of wistfulness and wondered, "Should I call her or is this just over?" In the end, she didn't.

NECESSARY GOOD-BYES

Sometimes a friend disappoints us so painfully and for so long, we have to let her go. How do you know when a friendship must be pruned? For some, it's when a relationship becomes a drain instead of a joy or a source of pain instead of solace.

"Friendships are like a marriage," said Laura. "There's give and take and compromise. Sometimes there comes a point where one person is doing more all the time. Sometimes it gets to the point where you explode and say, 'I've had enough.'"

Laura had considered Diane her best friend ever since they worked together as paralegals in Los Angeles in 1978. When Laura moved to Cleveland a decade ago, the friendship held fast. Laura's husband, who traveled frequently, mailed a free airline ticket to Diane every summer so she and Laura could travel to some exotic spot for a week. Laura flew to California twice for Diane's sons' bar mitzvahs.

But the first serious fissure appeared when Laura's father was dying. Diane was oddly detached through the ordeal. "I wanted her to call more and I wanted her to come here when he died," said Laura. "I would have done that for her. To me that's what a true friend is: someone who is physically and emotionally available."

Other cracks further weakened the foundation: Diane never thanked Laura's husband for the generous gifts of the plane tickets. While Laura would frequently call her friend, Diane usually responded by e-mail, which made Laura feel slighted. "She was too cheap to pick up the phone," Laura grumbles.

Then she invited Diane to her son and daughter's b'nai mitzvah, a combined bar and bat mitzvah. "She kept hemming and hawing. Then two weeks before she said, 'I'm not coming.' I was devastated. She's supposed to be my best friend and be with me on the biggest day of my life since my kids were born. It was both kids. It was going to be this big deal, and it was very important for me to have the people who were closest to me there. My dad was dead; my mother was dead. She ripped my heart out."

Three weeks after the event Laura received an e-mail from Diane asking about it. "I thought, 'You must be kidding. Where have you been?' She didn't even send a card. I thought about it for a month. I didn't answer her. Finally I wrote this long e-mail back saying what I thought friendship was. I said she hadn't been a friend of mine for a long time. I said it's been a one-way street for years." Diane didn't reply.

Six months of silence later, Laura received a note from Diane on her 50th birthday—the same day as Diane's daughter's birthday. "How could I not think of you?" Diane wrote. "I was wondering what you've been up to." She never addressed their break or Laura's grievance. Laura didn't respond. "I thought, what was the point? There was way too much ill will and history to a friendship that couldn't be resurrected."

Nor could Pam see a reason to preserve her relationship with Linda, who had been one of her closest pals for nine years. "I have a lot of patience and I'll stay there for a long time with someone," says Pam, 43, an at-home mom in Milwaukee. But the disappointments in Linda accrued until the friendship scale tipped irretrievably to one side. One of the first big letdowns was when Pam became pregnant after suffering an earlier miscarriage. Linda, who didn't have any children, brushed off her excitement. "Everyone's pregnant," Linda said flippantly. Then they fell out of touch for a while. When Pam realized how long it had been since they'd spoken, she called Linda's office to say hi, leaving a message with her secretary. Linda never returned the call.

Several months later, though, Linda phoned to have lunch. "She had just gotten a promotion. She was really nervous and she wanted to talk about it," Pam says. The day they were supposed to meet, however, Pam's father, who had been ill with cancer, was rushed to the hospital. Pam left a message for her friend, explaining that she was in the emergency room. Linda didn't respond. Eventually she contacted Pam, many months after Pam's father had died. Pam demanded, "Where have you been for the last year and a half?" Linda apologized, but for Pam it was too late. "She stopped being there for me when I thought she really would be. I didn't want to be hurt anymore," Pam explains. "It's like one of those punch dolls where you punch them down and they keep coming back in the same spot. It takes a while, but then you figure you should move out of the way."

It took me a long time to move out of the way with my former pal, Marissa. Even when a friendship is all give and no get, it can be hard to let it go. That's especially true when there isn't one dramatic breaking point. For years, I had invested 95 percent of the energy into holding together a decades-old relationship with Marissa. Often I wondered why I bothered, since it wasn't particularly satisfying anymore. I would have fallen over if she ever complimented me on anything or encouraged me in my work, though I did plenty of that for her. The friendship had been like driving hundreds of miles on a one-way road. Yet, dusty memories of a warmer, happier connection still tied me to her. And I felt a rapport with her almost unparalleled with anyone else. It scared me to think of losing it. I wondered if I could ever find it again. Then she canceled two dinner invitations to my house in a row without apology and nary a hint of regret. I didn't call her again, and guess what? She didn't call me.

Six months later, I scrawled a note to her asking what had happened to us. It sat addressed, stamped but unmailed, for weeks in the giant blue crockery bowl on my kitchen table. "Should I send it?" I asked my husband. "Do you really want that relationship?" he said, having heard me bemoan her neglect for years. No, I finally decided. A few weeks later, I tossed the note in the garbage. Untangling myself from her enabled me to focus on new people—in time, we recreated the bond that I'd had with my former friend, but without the angst. Hanging with a second-rate friend—like staying in a bad relationship with a guy—prevents you from finding a better one.

That's not to say the loss doesn't ache. Marissa might have been a lousy friend, but she was *my* lousy friend. After some women break up with their companions, they dream about them for years. One woman used to wake up with tears on her pillow after dreaming about her former friend.

"It's a lot like a death," says Pam, "but it's odd because that person isn't dead. You could pick up the phone and have lunch with them, but it's not the same. You cross a threshold and you can't go back." But there are no rituals to mourn the loss of a friend, nor formulas for finding a new one, she points out. "With a boyfriend you know exactly what to do. You do your grieving and you eat your ice cream and move on and start circulating again. You ask your friend, 'Do you know anybody for me?' It isn't that way with a friend. You can't put a personal ad in the paper. You can't go to your parents' friends and say, 'Do you have any daughters who might make a friend?'"

Before you dismiss someone for disappointing you, be clear on who is really a close friend. "We have best friends, good friends, casual friends," says Florence Isaacs, author of *Toxic Friends, True Friends*. "You may have a great time with your doubles tennis partner, but don't expect her to be there to help out when you're sick. Too often when people say 'so-and-so let me down,' it's not really that they let you down, but that you were expecting too much."

PRUNE CAREFULLY

Friends should not be abandoned lightly. Even the best relationships ebb and flow. Some days the conversation is like an exhilarating tennis rally; other days we can't hit the ball over the net. One friend and I cycle through varying degrees of closeness. We allow ourselves the elasticity.

Old friends cup our memories in their hands. They're irreplaceable vessels of our history. My friend Susan dove to the floor with me, choking with laughter, when bats flew into the Dairy Queen on our first job together in high school. We've retold that story about a hundred times. I remember her cute, guitar-playing eighth-grade boyfriend and the silver ID bracelet he gave her to go steady. We recall each other's parents before illness and age crept up.

Old friends are the graceful Queen Annes on the block. How soulless to live on a street full of teardowns. Certainly, no one should suffer in a toxic, unsatisfying friendship, but sometimes you just need to tread a rocky path or even a plain old boring one to come out on the other side. You may not have as much in common as you once did. But old relationships can be like your grandmother's silver candlesticks that you pull from the back of the cabinet and polish once a year on Thanksgiving. Not everyday stuff, but still worth having. And, who knows, maybe the lunch date you had with a new friend last week is the first page of a new, long history together.

12

Friendship Busters and Boosters

FRIENDSHIP is an art, and some women are natural Georgia O'Keeffes. They know how to apply the brushstrokes so their lives are lush with loyal friends. Other women weren't born with the ability. They gleaned the skills from their mothers and *their* friends.

But not everyone pays attention to the small gestures and thoughtful acts that burnish relationships. Those gestures are like steady deposits in a bank account. Over time they accrue and yield deeper trust and affection. And if a friend temporarily shifts into the debit column—as everyone does at times—you'll have a generous balance of goodwill to draw on. Someone may have disappointed you today, but it's not such a big deal if she's been a giving friend in the past. It's easier to let it go.

Sometimes, though, you do need to tell a friend that you're hurt, angry, or disappointed. It's a critical skill for any two people in an intimate relationship. If you can't hash out conflicts, your bond has a shorter life expectancy. But many troublesome behaviors, once you recognize them, can be avoided in the first place. If you limit the bad and multiply the good, you'll be able to hang on to your friends for a long time.

Friendship Wreckers

Some behaviors are guaranteed to corrode a connection. Neglect, habitual canceling, and jealousy are drops of acid that eat away at a friendship. Some women simply don't get what they're doing—or not doing—wrong. These are the Friendship Busters.

The serial canceller. Whenever I had a date with Marissa, she'd call that morning to cancel, arrange another date, then quash that one, too. She always had an excuse: she was tired from work, her floors were being buffed, her kid had a chess club meeting. By the third round, sometimes I was so annoyed I wanted to cancel just to let her know she wasn't the only person who had *more important things* going on.

Work deadlines loom, a kid sprouts chicken pox, the furnace croaks. Sometimes you can't get away. But canceling repeatedly—unless you're truly besieged—is insulting. It implies your life is more important than hers. After all, she's busy, but she saved the time slot for you. If you must ditch your date, express your regrets. "I'm so sorry. I was really looking forward to seeing you," is more palatable than a curt, "I have to cancel. I'm really busy at work."

Expecting an orange to be an apple. "Don't impose your standards on other people," advises Beth, 51, a graphic designer outside Phoenix. Her birthday is a big deal to her, but her oldest, dearest friend, Alisa, never calls or sends a card. "That's the way she is. If I expect one, I'm setting myself up for disappointment."

Ditto when Beth invited Alisa and her family for brunch. "She forgot to get back to me," sighs Beth. "I feel miffed, but I also know that's just her. She just doesn't remember to do some of those things. It feels personal, but it's not. I can make my peace with it or get myself tied up in knots. I value the friendship, so I let it go."

Alisa did, however, appear unexpectedly in the family waiting room both times Beth's husband was in surgery, once for a coronary bypass, another for prostate cancer. "You're not going to get her attention when you think you should. But you'll get it when you least expect it," Beth observes.

Understand your friend's limitations. We all have them and have to be generous with each other.

Emerald City. Jealousy pricks us all on occasion. Unpleasant, yes, but it won't doom a friendship if you face it. Deny its existence, however, and it will snake into your comments or actions.

Say a friend nabs a thrilling new job while you're glued to an unsatisfying one. Or she flashes a dazzling new engagement rock and you can't meet a decent guy to save your life. The challenge is acknowledging the rumble of envy while applauding the good news, allowing happiness for her to twine with the yearning for this great thing to happen to you, too. Not everyone succeeds all the time.

When Ellen, a divorced graphic designer, breathlessly told Lori that she was getting married, Lori didn't even say congratulations. "You're getting married and I can't even get a date," she whined. Lori was so self-absorbed, she couldn't be happy for her friend, just envious and self-pitying.

A friend's fortune seems to shine a harsh, unflattering light on our perceived shortcomings. Her gain seems like our loss. But it's not a competition. And envy is actually a useful emotion. It's a message from your deeper self, signaling your desires.

If you share that with the friend, she may even be able to help you stretch to fulfill for yourself what you admire about her — whether it's more challenging work or a snazzier image.

Here's how two friends actually drew closer in a situation in which jealousy could have easily sundered them. Jill had been struggling with infertility for years, when her closest pal, Lucy, gave birth to her first baby. Lucy and Jill recognized the delicacy of the event and its potential for rocking their relationship. But instead they used it to bolster each other.

If Jealousy Strikes

If jealousy is threatening your relationship with a pal, you have to face it before the friendship derails. Shelley Cohen, a personal and business coach in the Chicago area, offers these tips:

- First look within. If a friend's excitement about her success or good fortune is grating on you, ask yourself why. Is this an issue that you are sensitive about?

- Determine her motives based on your knowledge of her. If she's merely enthusiastic—and not trying to needle you—you may want to tolerate her excitement and be the supportive friend you'd want her to be for you. But if it's too painful, be honest. You could say, "I'm really happy for you, but this is difficult for me to listen to in light of what's going on in my life. I don't know if I can give you the support and response you need right now." There's a risk involved in being honest, but there's also a risk in putting on an act. You have to decide which is the bigger one.

- If you're certain she's being insensitive to you and knows what she is saying may be hurtful, you can call her on that. Try saying, "I want you to know that I am happy for you, but based on my own difficulties with this subject, which I know you are aware of, I'm having a real hard time listening to you talk about this all the time." Or, if you're really annoyed, you could zing, "When you talk about your new job all the time and you know I'm out of work, I feel you're not being sensitive to my feelings. I find myself wondering what your motives are."

After Lucy's baby was born, Jill came over to help several nights a week. It meant riding a train from her job in a distant suburb of Cincinnati to Lucy's city apartment, not an easy commute. "I was a mess," Lucy recalled. "I would be crying because I was so exhausted and strung out from being with a screaming baby all day. Jill would hold the baby and tell me it would get better." On her end, Lucy read up on infertility, was always available to listen to Jill's frustrations, and was careful not to talk endlessly about the baby when she called. "Lucy worked so hard to empathize with me even though she wasn't in that space. I always felt she knew what I was going through," Jill says. When Lucy became pregnant a second time, she was nervous about telling her friend. But Jill even accompanyied her for a sonogram.

Then Jill got pregnant. "It was one of the happiest days of my life," Lucy declares. When the baby was born, Lucy took a week off from her law office, bought a month's supply of formula and diapers (Jill had been superstitiously afraid to buy anything before the baby was born), and showed up at Jill's. She taught her how to dress and change her infant. She held the baby so Jill and her husband could eat dinner in peace. "I left my 2-year-old and 4-year-old home with my husband so I could help her with the baby," Lucy says. It was her great pleasure.

But what if you don't have a friend as sensitive as Lucy? That was Nicky's dilemma when she was struggling to conceive again after her first child was born. Several years of fertility treatments had failed. Then one morning her friend Isabelle called to announce she was pregnant. "She was very excited and went on and on about how easy it was for her to get pregnant," recalls Nicky, 48, a professor in Minneapolis. As her friend chattered away, Nicky felt as if she would scream or cry or both. "After being supportive, it got to be more than I could handle."

She realized she had to set some boundaries to protect herself. "I said to her, 'Honestly, I am very happy for you, but this is really hard for me to hear because of everything I've been through.' She was okay with it, but on some level she was probably disappointed," Nicky says. After that, Isabelle veered away from any mention of her pregnancy, but that was weird, too. "It seemed so unnatural," Nicky says. She finally told Isabelle, "This is ridiculous. I *do* want to know how you're doing." So they found a delicate balance in their conversations about the pregnancy, a middle ground that worked for both of them. "The good thing about sharing my feelings with her was that it reminded her of how sensitive the subject was for me," Nicky says.

It doesn't matter whether the issue inflaming jealousy is fertility, a pending wedding, or a great new job. Gently setting boundaries while assuring a friend we are happy for her, as Nicky did, benefits both people. It protects the sensitive one from being battered by endless conversations about a subject that is painful. It also lets the other person understand why her friend may not sound as wildly excited for her or as supportive as she'd expect.

But what if your pal seems to be rubbing your nose in her good fortune? At first April was delighted when Joan, 39, nabbed the first serious boyfriend of her life. In the beginning, she didn't mind that Joan blathered on about the wonderful new guy who brought her a big bouquet of flowers every time he came over. But as Joan endlessly bragged about his high-paying job, his big new house, their expensive dinners out, and the $600 massage table he bought her, the conversations began to rub April like a steel wool scouring pad. Joan—"who'd be the first to admit she's competitive," says April—perhaps not so innocently was chafing her friend's patch of thin skin. April's boyfriend, a doctoral student finishing his dissertation, didn't have the bucks for expensive gifts or a dozen roses every day. "I wanted to say, 'Will you shut up for a change!' On the one hand, you want to be patient; on the other hand, you want to smack her!" admits April, a 29-year-old book editor in New York. "It's my jealousy rearing its ugly head."

April found herself trying to compete by lauding her own boyfriend. Maybe he couldn't spring for a massage table, but he was no slouch in the rubdown department. "My shoulders are sore," April would sigh to Joan on one of their dates. "I know John will rub them for me when I get home." It irked her that she felt she needed to do that.

A couple things are likely at work here: Joan trying to make up for decades of insecurity because she lacked dates and, perhaps, a history of feeling jealous of April for "always having a boyfriend." Now Joan had a chance to lord her wealthy boyfriend over April's loving but financially pinched one.

Eventually, April stopped asking about Joan's boyfriend. Joan got the hint because she stopped talking about him to April, "but she still talks really loudly about him to others when I'm around," April says. "It's caused a rift. We're kind of in limbo right now."

What could April have done before the rift occurred? If she just wanted Joan to quit flapping her jaws about Mr. Wonderful at that moment, she could have steered the conversation to another track, perhaps by saying, "Enough about our boyfriends. Did you see [insert a recent movie title here]?" But if she wanted to set a boundary for future conversations, she might have tried, "I'm glad for you that this relationship is going so well, but hearing about him all the time is starting to be a little more than I can handle. Can we talk about something else?"

Hitting a Pothole

You're cruising down a well-paved friendship when suddenly you plunge into a crater-sized pothole. She said that your new condo was *tiny*. She canceled the third lunch date in a row. She didn't show up at your father-in-law's wake. You're fuming.

"In any close friendship the entire range of emotions that makes us human are going to rear their heads," says Harriet Lerner, a psychologist and the author of *The Dance of Anger*.

But those dark emotions scare us. We expect to spar with a husband or boyfriend. The bonds of a romance or marriage yank us back to repair the damage. Friendships, however, are bound only by the pleasure in each other's company. We're afraid they're assembled from glass—and not the shatterproof kind. So women tend to gulp down any furies that churn up, convinced if they reveal their anger or disappointment, the relationship will splinter into shards.

"There is an assumption among women that good female friendships should be conflict free," says Ruthellen Josselson, a psychotherapist and coauthor of *Best Friends: The Pleasures and Perils of Girls' and Women's Friendships*. "If we are good friends, we aren't supposed to be angry at each other. It comes from the way girls are socialized to be nice. If you aren't nice, then you are a bitch and no one is going to want to be your friend. There is the tyranny of niceness."

At the heart of most conflict between friends is not feeling valued or loved enough. "That's all very subtle," observes Josselson. "It's hard to say to somebody, 'I need you to love me more than you seem to be doing.'"

But burying anger or disappointment can infect a bond. Josselson offers a hypothetical example, in which Ann feels injured by Jane but doesn't talk to her about it. Instead, Ann thinks, 'Maybe Jane wasn't such a great person after all' or 'This wasn't the friendship I thought it was.' Now she's slower to return Jane's phone calls and is less available to get together. Jane senses Ann drifting, but doesn't understand why. 'What's wrong?' she asks. But so much time has passed, that 'the wrong' now seems trivial to Ann. But she doesn't feel as close to Jane anymore.

Having the moxie to unveil your nonwarm and nonfuzzy feelings can actually save a friendship. Lauren, a psychotherapist, told a friend she was hurt because the woman had virtually disappeared shortly after Lauren's mastectomy. It turned out the friend had been nursing her own injured feelings. When she had called to offer to bring dinner after the surgery, Lauren said she didn't need it. (She already had plenty of food from other people.) The friend had felt slighted. The women thrashed it out, cleared the air, and moved beyond it.

As did Kathleen and Sheryl. Sheryl was so consumed with her boyfriend, she kept forgetting her plans with Kathleen. Each canceled date wounded Kathleen ever deeper. Then Sheryl failed to show at Kathleen's 30th birthday party. When Sheryl called a day later to apologize, Kathleen didn't mince words. "I said, 'I don't know if I can be friends with you if you aren't going to participate in my life.' I said that I was really hurt. It was my 30th birthday party and it was a big deal. I told her what I expected out of friendship, someone who would not cancel on me all the time. If she didn't value the friendship, maybe we didn't need to be friends." Boyfriends come and go, Kathleen reminded her, "but a girlfriend is going to be around, hopefully, for a really long time."

Sheryl was jolted out of her boyfriend-induced stupor and affirmed that she cared about Kathleen. She also learned how to juggle her boyfriend (now ex-boyfriend, as Kathleen predicted) and friendships. "We're very close now. The reason is we learned how to resolve our conflicts and we know how important each of us is to the other," says Kathleen.

Indeed, sharing dissonant feelings with a friend builds up your relationship's muscle. It's like hoisting heavier weights in a workout. Whenever I've told a friend that something between us felt amiss, that very act affirmed that she was important to me. It also gave my friend permission to bring up anything that bothered her in the future. It's the equivalent of paving a new road, one that either of you can drive on.

Airing a concern also helps check out whether your worries are real or imagined. In *Between Women: Love, Envy, and Competition in Women's Friendships*, Luise Eichenbaum and Susie Orbach discuss how women project their unhealed hurts from their childhood relationship with their mothers onto female friends, imagining phantoms of anger and withdrawal where none actually exist. The friend who has fallen out of touch for a while may be merely distracted; she isn't necessarily angry at or pulling away from us. The friend whose greeting sounds tense or flat when we call her, instead of upbeat and welcoming, may just be stressed or depressed. It's rarely a reflection on how she feels about *us*.

Mending a Rift or Letting It Go

Not everything requires a heart-to-heart. How do you know whether to surf over anger or confront someone? How do you express your fury without igniting a fight or damaging the friendship? It's not always neat and it's not always easy. But with the right approach and two mature individuals, you should be able to pass through it and ultimately build a stronger connection. Here's a guide to finessing conflict.

1. Allow a cooling-off period if you're feeling injured by a pal. "Strike when the iron is cold," Lerner says wryly. "When you let time go by, you may realize that it's not that big a deal. Not everything has to be talked about. You don't have to address every little thing that irritates you about your friends."

2. Before confronting another person, confront yourself. Is your reaction being triggered by other things—you're upset about something else in your life, you're sensitive about a certain issue, you have PMS?

3. Ask yourself whether the friendship is close and open enough for an intimate conversation.

4. Pick your battles. Wait for issues that are truly damaging to the friendship. As Maggie, an attorney specializing in family law, asks herself, "How important is this to me? Is this the hill to die on? I try to let some stuff roll off my back. I try not to be too prickly."

5. If a cooling-off period passes and something is still bothering you, bring it up.

6. Choose a quiet place to talk. Discuss the problem calmly from the perspective of how you felt or perceived it. Use the word "I." For example, say, "I felt hurt and angry when you couldn't go out to lunch with me again this week," rather than accusing, "You blew me off for the third time in a month!" Don't begin by telling someone what she did to *you*. She will feel attacked and defensive. We're tempted to blather on when we're feeling emotional, but don't. Be concise and don't overtalk the issue.

7. If you are on the receiving end of a grievance, look honestly at your behavior and make amends if necessary. If you were wrong, say, "I'm sorry" (not the weaselly, "I'm sorry you were hurt"). And don't make excuses.

8. These heart-to-hearts won't work with everybody. If you already know a friend isn't able to talk about uncomfortable feelings, don't beat your head against the wall. Navigating conflicts only succeeds when two people care about the relationship and are capable of working through a problem.

9. What if you've already had a blowup? "The issue may fade away," says Lerner. Or, she suggests, you can say, " 'I miss you. I know we had a lot of intensity.' Sometimes the event doesn't need to be processed. Sometimes you may repair the damage by offering a sincere apology for your part, even if you think your part is only 18 percent." When Rebecca and Kristin—who had stopped speaking after a fight—spied each other at a party, Rebecca tentatively approached her old friend at the dessert buffet. "You know, I still love you," she said. End of fight.

Surviving a Fight

Conflict is messy, awkward, and usually survivable. One conversation may be enough to repair a rift. But it also may be only the first step in a longer process of healing. Friends may have to tolerate some discomfort for a while. It's like entering a tunnel: dark, dark, dark, then light.

Diane and Jackie wondered if they ever would make it through the tunnel. The survival of their friendship is a testament to the value of riding out the rough parts. The women were longtime pals who created and shared the job of executive director of a nonprofit organization in the Chicago area. "We were almost like a couple, Frick and Frack," recalls Diane. When one woman showed up at a function, people looked around for the other one. They shot each other conspiratorial looks in meetings with bores. They were the perfect yin and yang of managers. Diane was detail oriented for day-to-day operations; Jackie envisioned the future.

About three years into the job, Diane's rocky marriage fell apart. She was emotionally raw and terrified about the future. Right about that time, Jackie was offered a new job as executive director of a national women's organization. She felt tugged between loyalty to Diane and a terrific career opportunity that was a better fit than her current job. Ultimately, she decided to grab the new post. "I realized I needed to do this. I knew it was going to be difficult for her. I felt very badly about it," Jackie says.

So did Diane. "This was the last thing I needed," Diane says. "I was so angry. I felt betrayed and abandoned. She was pulling out on something that was important to me." Diane worried that she couldn't manage their job on her own.

Because Jackie had given several months' notice, the two women still had to work together. Diane's anger crackled through the office, her voice brittle and testy. "I never let a moment pass to let her know how I felt. Anytime I could take a cheap shot at her, I did. I was going through a hellish time. I couldn't see beyond that," Diane says.

But Jackie never hooked into her fury. "I was trying to be patient. I'd tell myself, 'Okay, I'm going to deflect everything she's saying to me. I'll let it bounce off me. I'm not going to take the way she's acting personally.' I understood her reaction."

Not that she wasn't affected by the storm. "There were some horrible days. Nobody likes being yelled at and having somebody they care about really angry with them," Jackie says. But she recognized that Diane's venting was healthy for their survival. "A lot of people, when they are angry with each other, don't feel comfortable shouting with each other and they can't get past it."

"She let me pummel her for a long time," Diane says with awe. "Jackie kept saying, 'Diane, you can do this by yourself. You don't need me.' She's an amazing friend. She kept encouraging me."

As Diane began sailing solo in her job, her rancor drained away. "I finally realized what Jackie was doing was absolutely the right choice for her," she says. One morning soon after she called Jackie to ask, "Do you want to have lunch?" Jackie could almost hear the clink of icicles crashing to the ground.

It's Never Too Late to Make Up

Ideally, friends reconcile soon after a fight. The older a rift, the wider it grows until it hardens into a kind of permanent continental drift. The anger has usually burned away, the incident that provoked it bleached from memory. But former friends don't know how—or are afraid—to reach across the breach.

But it's never too late to make up. Those that take the leap may rediscover a relationship that's only been on ice and can be quickly thawed. Some wave the white flag through e-mail—which seems less risky than a phone call. That's what Jill finally did after wondering for seven years how her old pal Melissa was doing since they "broke up."

Here's what Jill wrote to me in an e-mail about their relationship and its repair:

> Melissa and I met in our first year of college in New York City. We became fast friends and later shared an apartment. Melissa was one of the few girlfriends I had who I felt truly understood me.
>
> Then I began a relationship with the man who is now my husband. I spent less and less time at the apartment

Melissa and I shared. I guess she felt abandoned by me and after increasing tension, we had an explosive fight. I was furious that she seemed unwilling to accept my new relationship or support my happiness.

It has been almost seven years since Melissa and I "broke up." My anger has completely faded and I have frequently wondered how she was doing. About a month ago, I typed her name into an Internet search engine and located her e-mail address. Fearful she would reject me after all these years, I sent her an e-mail anyway. I apologized for our fight and told her how much I missed her. A few hours later, I received a touching and beautiful note from her. That evening we were on the phone, talking as though no time or bitterness had passed between us.

We are both ashamed of how we treated each other all those years ago and saddened by how much time we have lost. But now we're happily catching up and arranging a visit. I feel blessed to have her back. What would I have done differently? Talked with her after that explosion, swallowed my own pride and anger for the sake of our relationship. Better late than never, I suppose.

Of course, if you don't know her e-mail address, you could always write a letter or leave a message on her answering machine at an hour when you think she won't be home. (The latter is highly risky, though, if she has kids. They could erase it, as some kids do, and she might never get the message.) If you're feeling especially brave, slip on your armor and call when you expect to catch her. What's the worst that can happen in any of these scenarios? She won't respond to your overtures. You'll feel bruised, sure, but you'll rebound fast. Because ultimately it won't change anything. She hasn't been in your life anyway; at least now you have closure and you don't have to wonder "what if?" On the optimistic side, she might have been thinking about you, too. Your courage could rekindle a once-valued friendship.

How to Feed a Friendship

On the flip side of the Friendship Busters are the Boosters, the acts that help a relationship flourish. These deeds are the equivalent of friendship vitamins. They ensure your friendship will grow new rings around its core, like a graceful old oak.

1. **Pay attention.** Keep tabs on the significant events in a friend's life. Did her daughter just head off to college? Call to see how she's holding up and invite her over for coffee. Did her dad have bypass surgery? Check in.

   A Thoughtful Act: Reese's mother became seriously ill and was rushed to the hospital in the midst of her father's radiation treatments. "My friend, Kimberly, called me every day for a week to ask me how I was doing, not just my parents," Reese says. "It wasn't just a five-minute conversation, it was half an hour. She spent the time even though it was over Christmas, and she had her whole family in town." Reese says she learned how to better support her other friends from Kimberly's example.

2. **Exercise your dialing finger.** Friendship thrives on knowing the minutiae of each other's lives. You can't know them unless you stay in touch. Don't quibble about whose turn it is to call.

3. **Crack open your date book.** The happiest women wedge spaces into their week for pals no matter how busy they are. They meet for muffins before work, hit side-by-side treadmills at the health club, sashay out for dinner on a weeknight. Make it a nonnegotiable date.

4. **Raise a flute of champagne.** Sure, we need people when

life clops us between the eyes. But it's just as important to cheer the victories. Did she finally finish her master's thesis or nab a promotion? Take her out to lunch or send her a note.

5. **Rain compliments.** Most of us don't get a lot of strokes—from our boss, our family, or our kids. That's what friends are for. I know a woman who makes me feel gorgeous and brilliant—well, at least attractive and capable—nearly every time we talk. How could you not love her?

   A Thoughtful Act: Nina, a doctor from St. Louis with three kids, left this message on the answering machine of a friend who had recently started her own business: "I'm really proud of you and how hard you're working. I know you'll do so well!"

6. **Show up for happy and sad events.** Friendship means sharing significant events together. When I was going through a divorce, my oldest pal showed up the night before I had to move out of my condo to help me pack. I was so shaky, I would have left behind half my possessions if it weren't for her. The same friend always comes to my daughter's musicals. Nina cancelled all her appointments at work and hopped a plane to comfort a friend at her mother's funeral. Another pal of mine showed up at my door to pay a condolence call after my beloved guinea pig of eight years died. We sat at the kitchen table and cried about lost pets, past and present.

7. **Light some birthday candles.** People are touched when someone remembers their birthday. It doesn't have to be a grand gesture—just a phone call or a card. My New Year's resolution was to finally make a list of close friends' birthdays and hang it next to my calendar.

8. **If something is really important to you, say so.**
   Speaking of birthdays, one of my closest, oldest friends
   forgot to call me on one of my most significant ones. I
   was particularly sensitive about this milestone. When I
   saw her several days later, she said she had been distracted by her kitchen renovation. "Your new counters
   are more important than me!?!" I wanted to shout. I tried
   to forget it, and maybe a bigger person could have, but it
   gnawed at me. Finally, a month later, I told her I was
   really hurt. "It means a lot to me that you pay attention
   to this day," I said. There is not another nonfamily
   person in the world I would have had the nerve to say
   this to. "I'm really glad you told me," she said. "I'm flat-
   tered that it means so much to you that I remember."

9. **Gift rap.** Nina is always delivering impromptu, "no special reason" gifts to her friends and even their kids. She
   buys books about writing for one woman who wants to
   become an author and ladybug stationery for a friend's
   daughter who covets all things ladybug. "It tells you
   you're important enough that someone went out of their
   way to do something for you," says Nina.

   Kimberly, a business consultant (and Reese's caring
   friend), hands out no-special-occasion baskets brimming
   with her homegrown tomatoes, squash, fresh herbs, or a
   loaf of freshly baked banana bread. "I try to make the gift
   fit the friend," she says. My daughter just dropped off a
   quart of chocolate ice cream for a girlfriend who had
   braces put on. She already understands the value of a
   present.

10. **Return calls and e-mails promptly.** Try to respond
    within a day or two. Lengthy delays or not calling back
    can chafe feelings. If you're too busy for a conversation,

leave a brief message on her machine explaining you'll be in touch when you're able.

11. **Make peace with imperfection.** "I have a friend who is a big procrastinator, a friend that's always late, and a friend that brags and doesn't give you kudos," says Samantha, the attorney. "But I accept their faults and work around that. They have a good core. I talk too much. I'm sure my friends put up with that."

12. **Roll up your sleeves.** In a crisis, offer a ride to the doctor's, transportation for her kids, baby-sitting, dinner, grocery shopping, laundry washing, or whatever she needs.

13. **Practice artful listening.** Listening well is a skill. That's because the overriding instinct is to try to fix our friends' problems—or interrupt and badger them with ours.

One summer afternoon I sipped iced tea with a friend, mourning my teenage daughter's inevitable ripping away. I just wanted the friend to murmur, "Yeah, it's hard" or "I understand." Instead, she peppered me with advice. As my irritation bloomed, I also felt an unpleasant startle of recognition. *I* did that. I heard the echo of my advice-giving voice in hers. She and I had noble intentions, but we were feeding our own need to help. I felt ashamed of my past listening transgressions and vowed to can the counselor rap.

I'm learning from a few people who are terrific listeners. They sit quietly with an occasional empathetic nod or cluck, ask a few questions to help clarify the situation and later, gently offer the perspective of their own experiences.

"I used to want to dismiss somebody's feelings or offer suggestions," admits Nina. "When my friend's son became paralyzed, I couldn't fix that. I started to learn to listen. I say, 'You're entitled to those feelings.' It's more comfortable. I used to spend so much time trying to fix their problems."

Sometimes we do want advice or another opinion. When that's the case, we usually ask. Or, as Kimberly says, "You can hear in a conversation when people just need a safe harbor. But you also might hear a little voice that says, 'What do you think?' I listen for that entree and offer what my thoughts are."

The Nicest Thing My Friend Ever Did for Me

Life is frantic, and the knowledge that someone paused in the midst of the craziness to do something special for us shimmers for a long time. The women in the following vignettes wrote to me to share special memories, some of them decades old but still fresh in their minds. That's how much these acts meant to them. None of these gestures was expensive or time consuming, but they were appreciated more than the good-deed doers probably ever knew.

Lisa and I are both stay-at-home moms with kids the same age. We were to meet one morning for coffee (a real treat!) while our kids were at school. That morning, my oldest was home sick and so I had to call and cancel. We were both so bummed because this date had been on the calendar for a while. It is so rare that we have time to catch up with each other. About 30 minutes later, she showed up at my door, a caramel latte in hand, and said, "Let's have a phone date!" and went home. While my daughter slept, we chatted on the phone, had our coffee, and caught up with each other. It really touched me. She's a wonderful friend. [Grace, 37, an at-home mom]

When I had cancer, I complained to a friend long distance over the phone that I had lost all my hair and I felt ugly.

She sent a get well card saying "Cheer Up!" with a black negligee. She was saying it doesn't matter about the hair, you're still beautiful. [JEWEL, 47, A TV PRODUCER]

I have this friend with these little wine glasses I like with engraved flowers on them. She only has two. She always serves wine in them when I go to her house. She was at an antique store and found four similar glasses with a decanter. She bought those for me. It was so out of the blue. She could have kept them for herself, but she thought about me. That is the nicest gift I've ever gotten. [VIVIAN, 37, AN AT-HOME MOM]

Twenty years ago, I had an 18-month-old and had just given birth to my second child. We were moving 10 days later. A friend called and asked what day the movers were coming to pack me. She said, "I'll be over at noon with lunch." She got on the bus, in Manhattan, with her baby and a picnic basket, and brought lunch. It was something very special and kind. She didn't say, "What do you need?" she said, "I'm going to do this for you." Often people ask is there anything they can do to help. It is not a terribly helpful question. You don't want to ask for something, but it's so lovely when somebody just does it. [ROBIN, 40, A RABBI]

We all know women who are friend magnets. People are drawn to them like hummingbirds to nectar. They make new friends with a silky ease and hang on to old ones forever. We may envy their magic, but we can cast the same spell ourselves. It's simple. Be an intentional friend, one that pays careful attention to a pal's life and needs. Treat a friendship like the gift that it is.

13

A Gang of Your Own

꿈

Why You Need Community

ON AN episode of *The Simpsons*, Helen Fielding, the author of *Bridget Jones's Diary*, makes a surprise appearance at Marge's book club. But before anyone realizes who she is, a member blurts out, "Let's all tell why we didn't have time to read the book." Fielding stomps out.

Okay, sometimes women in a book club don't read the book, including me. But they still leave work early and/or fling a pizza at their kids to make a 7:30 meeting about a novel they didn't crack open. That's because the prospect of chewing on good literature isn't the only draw of the night. It's at least equal parts desire to belong to a group and hang out with the same people once a month.

Many of us crave community—a critical nutrient that's often missing in our spartan social diet of individually focused lives. The wildly popular TV show *Friends* is funny, sure, but much of its enormous appeal is in the tribe of loving pals whose lives are inextricably intertwined. Many of the millions of viewers no doubt yearn for a cozy group like the one they see on television. They can hit the remote every week and catch some of the reflected glow.

One telling measure of the hunger for community emerged when an article about a committed women's friendship group in Eugene, Oregon, appeared in *Health* magazine. Women from as far away as Texas called one of the members to say they were considering picking up and moving to Eugene so they could join the group.

One-on-one friendships—while vital—are not the same as community. Community is about numbers—a gang that bikes 20 miles through the woods every Sunday or knits sweaters on Tuesday nights in a coffee shop. Groups anchor us. The banter is often breezy, sort of friendship-lite. But there's nothing inconsequential about feeling embraced and accepted by a clan. It assures us that we're likeable. That's powerful stuff.

In past generations, community often sprang up naturally in neighborhoods or from our extended families. My mother had her weekly bridge game and coffee klatches. I still remember a neighbor, Lee, appearing on her front lawn one broiling summer afternoon with a tray of iced coffees in frosty glasses to pass out to Jan (my mom), Anita, and Roz, who had stepped out of their split-levels for some friendly gossip. The women even grocery shopped together because only one of them owned a car.

Simply put, we're on our own more often now. The old structures don't function the way they used to. We hurtle through life and don't have time to get to know the people on our block. Many of us are flung far from parents, siblings, and cousins. Work friendships fracture as companies slash budgets and employees, and more people are isolated in home offices as telecommuters or in home-based businesses. Even marriage is a wobbly source of both companionship and social webbing. According to the U.S. Census Bureau, the proportion of never-married women in their early thirties has more than tripled in the past three decades, from 6 percent to 22 percent of the female population. Never-married and divorced women and men comprise a bigger chunk of the population than they did thirty years ago. Clearly, we need to craft our own tribes.

But I'm Not a Joiner

Forging new clans isn't so easy. Plenty of us are reluctant joiners. I quit Brownies in second grade and couldn't wait to escape the sorority I pledged in college. As a journalist, I shunned professional associations. When I was desperate to meet people on a return move to Chicago, I dipped my toe into a religious-based women's group and yanked it out. Nothing ever felt right. And yet, on weekends away from work, I often wrestled with an emptiness that individual pals, a boyfriend, and later, even a husband and child couldn't fill. I felt strangely untethered, but I didn't know why. I didn't know that I was missing a community.

My colleagues at a Dallas newspaper gave me my first taste of belonging. Perhaps my neediness (not knowing a soul in town) made me more willing to knock over the barricades I usually flung up to avoid the overtures of a group. We threw barbecues on weekends and dropped off carryout Chinese food if someone was sick. For me, it was the first gang that fit. I was shocked at how good it felt.

NOT A FRIVOLOUS PURSUIT

Scientific research echoes my experience. Psychologist Belle Liang and others have found that women who have a sense of belonging to a larger community or group are less lonely, depressed, and anxious. Hanging out with a gang, in some ways, is even more important for women than individual friendships, suggests Liang, an assistant professor at Boston College.

"There is something about being in a group that helps people to feel more at an equilibrium," she explains. "In some ways, while you gain your identity, you also lose your identity and become part of something bigger than yourself, less of a self-consciousness and more of a collective focus. It really grounds a person."

The Pleasures of Friendship-Lite

While you may be looking for a deep connection, don't expect soul-searching chats and intimate relationships in most large groups. Conversation often skims the surface or swirls around an activity, which can be a pleasant change from the intensity of individual friendships. And once you're comfortable in a gang, you can relax. You don't have to keep proving yourself. A friend once apologized to me because she was in a funk and was worried that she wasn't good company. She obviously felt some self-induced pressure to be entertaining and upbeat. I told her our friendship wasn't based on her liveliness quotient. But being with just one other person does demand a higher output of emotional energy.

Ginger, 45, who owns a landscape business in St. Louis, appreciates the more diffuse focus when she's with her gang of three old high school buddies. "You don't always have to be on center stage all the time. I can sit back and listen. I don't always have to be up and perform," she explains.

A contagious energy whips around a circle of women, inspiring bouts of raucousness. On one "girls only" vacation weekend, a woman cranked up her boom box and spontaneously taught her gang to dance the Electric Slide. "We were laughing, carrying on, going nuts," she recalls. "One-on-one, that wouldn't happen, the whole atmosphere of everyone joining in, being silly. It was great!"

Once a circle is established, it requires less effort to maintain than individual relationships. You know you'll always meet the first Monday of every month to talk about short stories, for example. No one has to make a phone call. A group is also relatively stable. "There's a comfort that comes from knowing if one person leaves, there's still a group," says Rebecca Adams, a professor of sociology at the University of North Carolina at Greensboro, who researches and writes about friendship. "With one friend, you have a more fragile relationship. It only takes that one person deciding to end the relationship for that part of your life to go away."

Your friendship menu needs a range of both intimates and acquaintances. Think of them as concentric circles. You should have an inner ring of close friends with whom you can share and who will rally around you in an emergency. And you need an outer band of casual friends and social groups that offer companionship and a sense of belonging.

You Don't Have to Look Very Far

While this chapter targets community you create yourself, that doesn't mean you should ignore one important source right in your own backyard. You may not have a lot in common with your neighbors, but it's important to have a solid relationship with them. When my family and I had to leave town quickly for a funeral, it was a comfort to know I could ask Suzy to feed my guinea pig, Shelley to collect my newspapers, and Betty to grab the mail. We call each other in emergencies and train an unobtrusive eye on each other's lives through our living room windows.

Such as the night a ponytailed, tattooed motorcyclist roared into Shelley's driveway and offered her teenage son a ride on his gleaming Harley. Shelley wasn't home, but her 74-year-old next-door neighbor spied the scene and marched over to demand the stranger's identity. She also informed her 16-year-old neighbor he wasn't getting on that bike. (Turned out the Harley rider was a lawyer and a family friend, but Shelley appreciated her neighbor's concern.)

These good relations take cultivating. I drop off occasional spaghetti dinners for Betty since she's been widowed. One day I heard hammering in my backyard and saw my other next-door neighbor, Brian, repairing my wooden fence, which had toppled over, unbeknownst to me, into his yard after a storm. That afternoon I brought over a chocolate layer cake with "Thank You!" spelled out in blue frosting. Shelley and I grab lunch or dinner every few months to catch up. We all exchange small holiday gifts: Betty delivers homemade taffy, Ron his ultrarich butter cookies. Without my neighbors, I'd feel terribly alone. They're my security blanket.

Even so, neighbors reside mostly in the background. You need a center stage for your own community, people whom you see regularly, to create a reassuring baseline in your week or month. When these people recognize and greet you—whether it's in a meeting or at the grocery store—it says you matter.

Different Tiers

So how do we kindle this sense of fellowship that often eludes us? An ideal group may already exist, waiting for you to discover it. But for many of us, community requires an act of creation, a purposeful weaving together of women, or women and men, around an activity, discussion, or charity. Here are stories of women who did exactly that. Each of them sculpted a group, from people they already knew or strangers — or both. Here also are people who found an existing circle that worked for them. Perhaps you're a birder, biker, or knitter. Perhaps there's a weekly Bible class at your church or women's group at your synagogue. The Internet is a terrific source to find local groups catering to every passion and interest (type your interest, say, knitting groups, into Google.com and see what comes up). The first step to cementing a sense of community is simply showing up, again and again.

THE URBAN TRIBE

Alexa is an avid matchmaker. But she doesn't fix up romantic partners; she links people she thinks could be pals. "I love it when people I think are cool meet each other. People hardly set each other up in terms of friendship, and I think that's so much more important than romance," says the 33-year-old Chicago divorce attorney.

One night, Alexa invited three men and four women she adored — but most of whom didn't know each other — to come to dinner. Their instant rapport awed her. "I looked at this table after a couple hours of us eating dinner and laughing and thought, 'My God, we all get along so well. I've got to make sure we all hang out.'" So she invited them to meet for drinks at a new bar the following week. They zipped back seven enthusiastic e-mails confirming they'd be there. Thus, Alexa spliced together her urban tribe. They began meeting en masse every few weeks for Friday dinner out, Sunday night movies at someone's house, birthday parties, Thanksgiving dinner, and even a New Year's trip to Paris. Over time, the group began to think of each other as a family away from home.

But one of the members, Trista, resisted that family notion until she had a near-fatal bike accident. When she regained consciousness in the hospital, she was surrounded by every member of her posse, as well as her actual family. Police were able to contact her parents by punching one of the preset numbers on her cell phone to reach her pal, Jeff. He remembered the small Nebraska town where Trista grew up and where her parents still lived. Stunned by the devotion of her friends, Trista decided they were, indeed, her surrogate kin. "It makes me feel peaceful. You know there's that stability in your life. We joke about how when we're old, we'll be in a nursing home together."

Indeed, that constancy in a life freighted with uncertainty is why so many singles form urban tribes, says Ethan Watters, who wrote a book on the phenomenon, *Urban Tribes: A Generation Redefines Friendship, Family, and Commitment*. Jobs change, apartments change, lovers change, but the tribe remains. "No one will fire you from the tribe," he says.

"We're thrown into large cities without our kin and we're expected to survive on our own for five or ten years," Watters explains. "Our reaction is to form connections and form those connections into groups. This is what humans do. This is ingrained in our nature."

Watters did it, too, after breaking up with a girlfriend when he was 26. "I was feeling lonely and lost, feeling the looseness of my city life, the lack of momentum," Watters recalls. He needed something he could depend on. So he told his friends he would be at a certain restaurant every Tuesday night at 7:30. Anybody who wanted to come could show up. They did; sometimes three people, sometimes as many as 20. Those Tuesday night dinners spawned an annual houseboat trip, a Las Vegas jaunt on Halloween, and other rituals that lend shape and momentum to their lives. E-mail lubricates their socializing, because if someone had to make a dozen phone calls to arrange an activity, it might not happen.

But posses can have a downside, especially when a member tries to integrate a new significant other into the existing crew. Then territorial insecurities and jealousies may boil up. "The group can be brutal at times," says Molly, 32, a divorce attorney who is part of Alexa and Trista's tribe. "I was the first one to start dating someone. It took a long time for them to accept him. Everyone looked at him like, 'How long is he going to be around?' They pretty much ignored him. They really hoped that he would go away and they'd have my full attention again. They'd say, 'Why does he always have to come?'"

It was a stressful time for Molly, who tried to carve out time alone with her friends to make sure they didn't feel slighted and separate time with her boyfriend. She only included him in the group occasionally. "It was a terrible balancing act," she says.

But it was worth it to her so she didn't lose them. She'd seen many of her other friendships wane as female pals married, moved to the suburbs, and wrote her off. The tribe, while possessive, had gilded her life with so many people and activities she enjoyed—plays, picnics, volleyball, biking, and traveling—she was willing to put up with their peevishness.

Over time and as other members of the group started dating, Molly's boyfriend was accepted into the fold. "Now they want their significant others in the group. They've evolved past their clannishness to be more open and accepting," Molly says.

Boyfriends aside, group dynamics can still get sticky. "There are jealousies every once in a while when you find out someone made dinner for two people and didn't invite the whole group," says Trista. "I feel a pang, but I realize not everything can be a big group affair. I crave my one-on-one time with these people, too, so I get over it."

"It's not always smooth sailing. We have arguments," Alexa acknowledges. Sometimes they're trivial, like disagreements over where to eat dinner. Sometimes they're more serious, like when several members told another one what they really thought about her boyfriend. But like a family, they stick together until the irritation fades.

But it's a family they choose. They skimmed off a few original members whose behaviors they didn't like. One was a selfish woman. "She'd always say, 'Can you pick me up?' which is not a big deal, but then she'd never offer herself. She was just a very me, me, me kind of person," says Alexa. A man was kicked out for being too demanding, taking advantage of people, and always expecting to get his way. The tribe simply stopped including the undesirables in their e-mails. "They were very angry. It's an awkward situation, but it was that or put up with bullshit," says Alexa.

As Alexa gazes into the future, she realizes the tribe will necessarily reshape itself as members marry. "I wonder, will it be the same with a spouse or will they have kids and you'll never see them again?" But she's hopeful their bonds are elastic. "I'm confident even if they have kids they'll still stay in contact."

KNITTING TOGETHER IN MORE WAYS THAN ONE

Blowing snow whipped her face, but Kate clutched her knitting needles and trudged to the coffee shop, yellow light streaming from its windows like a beacon on an inky night. Even an Illinois snowstorm couldn't stop her from venturing out. This is her oasis: women sprawled around tables and couches with a rainbow of sweaters, scarves, afghans, and baby hats unfurling from their knitting needles. They are the women of Stitch'n'Bitch.

The group was started by a woman who tried knitting as a

stress reliever from her job as a Web designer. With only her two cats as company, she didn't want to knit at home, and so Stitch'n'Bitch was born. (To find out if a group's in your area, go to www.stitchnbitch.org.)

The first night, Kate was so nervous she cased out the group but didn't join them. The second time she greeted them in a small voice, "Hi, I'm a knitter." They made room for her. Kate's shyness melted by the third gathering. "The knitting is your introduction to sit there and break into the conversation," she says.

Some of her other friends had thought it was strange that she, a 26-year-old woman, liked to stay home in her apartment and knit while they caroused in bars. Not so here. "It validates that I like to knit and it's not uncool," she says.

"I was searching for something like this for the longest time. I was feeling somewhat isolated," says Kate, who works in a small jewelry company. When she first heard about the group on a TV show, she said she literally gasped in delight. "Unless you have built-in friendships from high school or college, it's hard to meet people with a similar interest," she says.

Her new group fits like, well, a hand-knit mitten. Conversation among the women—in their 20s to 40s and from varying careers—floats easily from current events to whether a member has found a new job. They may ask each other for guidance on tricky spots in their patterns. Sometimes the only sound is the gentle clicking of needles.

"I don't hang out with people in any other situation. Maybe this is the beginning of getting a close friendship with one of the girls. That might develop," Kate says hopefully. "Whatever happens during the week, Tuesdays I will go relax, have some coffee, and chitchat with people who have a common interest." She's also finishing up the sleeves on a black alpaca cable-knit cardigan.

SPOKES AND FOLKS

Sunday mornings at 8:30, Marie straps on her helmet, fills her water bottle, and bikes to the forest—ignoring the persistent ache of rheumatoid arthritis in her legs. At the paved trail she meets three friends for a sweaty 20-mile ride—rain or shine. (In the winter, they fitness walk together.) The fresh air and exercise are exhilarating, but the big payoff is a "sense of renewable friendship," says Marie, 58, who coordinates public relations for a Midwestern university. They head to a botanic garden where they refuel with muffins and coffee in the cafe, then circle back home. Nobody complains that Marie keeps a slower pace.

When the women launched their Sunday ride five years ago, Marie was best friends with one of them and more casual buddies with the other two. But they've all drawn closer as a result of their weekly ritual. "You can rotate who you talk to. You're not exclusively with one person. It widens my world a little. It's a good support system for me," says Marie. Without this routine, Marie admits it's unlikely she'd take the time to catch up with each woman every week.

When Marie's daughter left for college, she immersed herself in groups—bridge, book, and biking. "I was making a postchild life for myself. It connected me more with the people around me and the town. It gave me definite social dates I wouldn't normally have and more of a sense of personal community."

WHETHER YOU READ THE BOOK OR NOT

I have barely finished chewing my dinner before I fly out of the house into a pelting rain. I leave behind a sink full of dishes and my then-10-year-old daughter, who is uneasy staying alone for an hour until her father gets home. But I brush away the guilt, scribbling the phone number where I'll be on a scrap of paper. My monthly book club meeting is a powerful draw.

In Sally's living room, I nestle into the corner of the couch as the leader poses a question about the novel we all—well, most of us—have read. None of the women are my close friends, yet after several years together I feel a niche here. When I bump into other members in the grocery store or the halls of our kids' school we ask, "Have you read the book? What did you think?" Over the tomatoes, someone may declare, "I hated it!" or "I stayed up till 2 A.M. reading. I couldn't put it down." It's the conversation pool, our common thread.

Lisa started the club because she felt isolated amidst the women living within a few blocks of each other in our hamlet. She knew we needed something to bind us. So she invited a handful of women to her house, and they've been coming to each other's homes ever since. The only rule: don't make a big fuss over refreshments so nobody feels pressured. The woman who laid out a delectable spread of shrimp and sushi was gently asked to scale back in the future. A different person organizes the group every year. The faces have changed as some original members dropped out and new ones joined. One constant, though, is the enthusiastic postbook socializing. When I hosted a meeting, I had to end it a bit early at 9:30 so my daughter could go to sleep. When I climbed into bed nearly an hour later, women were still standing on the sidewalk, talking in the moonlight.

CREATING A COMMITTED COMMUNITY

The story has become almost legendary among women in Eugene, Oregon. Ellen Weaver was having coffee after a movie with her friend, Martha Snyder, when they began fretting about their bank accounts in old age. "How will I have any money when I am 65?" worried Ellen, then in her late thirties and a single mom who cobbled together odd jobs to support herself and her daughter. "That's okay, we can be bag ladies together," joked Martha, who was also single. Ellen asked her then next-door neighbor if she wanted to join them. "We will get old together and take care of each other," she proposed.

Thus, Ellen assembled a circle of women called Bag Ladies of the World, or BLOWs. While practical and emotional support may be a happy by-product of other groups, this one was organized specifically with that in mind.

Now Ellen is married; some Bag Ladies, who were hitched when the group started, are now divorced. The underlying belief: men may come and go, but the BLOWs last forever. Its nearly 20-year history reflects all that's good and all that's troublesome in a long-term friendship group.

To solder the BLOWs together in the beginning, the women gathered for monthly Sunday brunches, skiing, and crafts, like making plaster casts of their faces and breasts (which they wore in a town parade!). When the original group hit 13 members, another BLOWs circle was formed, then another and another, until five had blossomed in the Eugene area. Each group has a name like Crones of a Feather or The Wicked Aunties. They call each other sisters, as in "I saw sister Carmen today." Of course, it's said in a joking manner, but also in a serious, affectionate way, Ellen says.

Turns out the women didn't have to wait for old age to watch out for each other. When Ellen, now 56, shattered her ankle after she toppled off her bike, BLOWs members rallied. They perched by her bedside at the hospital after surgery, donated crutches, and delivered home-cooked meals to her house. Everybody knew about Ellen's ankle because the first woman who found out launched a calling tree.

When Karen, a member of another BLOWs group, had a

Caesarean section, women arrived at her house for three, 2-hour shifts every day the first week. They knew her husband had to return to work right after the baby was born and couldn't help during the day. The BLOWs cared for the baby and made dinner, so Karen could catch up on sleep. The second week someone showed up once a day to help. "I was overwhelmed by how kind they were to me. It's an intentional family," Karen says. "I felt like I had somebody I could count on. It was the way we used to live when aunties and grandmas were around to help you raise your children."

It seemed positively idyllic, at least at first. "I thought we were all going to live happily ever after and group-hug all the time and sit around and laugh and joke and never have any conflicts, like anybody who was a newlywed," admits Karen. "But as time progresses, everybody comes to the table with her own set of baggage."

Some people were "hardship hogs," she says, bringing more of their troubles to the group than others. Personalities clashed. One woman complained that not enough people had visited or brought dinner after she had minor surgery. Another excoriated the group for what she perceived as its shortcomings at every meeting.

None of this surprises Ellen Weaver. "It's like family," she explains. "Who gets along with their family all the time? There are some members of your family you're closer to than others."

Karen stresses that women need realistic expectations about what a group like this can ultimately provide. "You can't expect it to solve all your needs. You have to be part of a group and an independent person at the same time. You can't go into a group with your emotional baggage and expect it to be your bellboy," she says.

And closeness with a circle may ebb and flow. While Karen

remains a member, she doesn't feel as tied to the group as in the past. But she can feel its invisible presence in her life, ready to catch her if she falls. "I know if I came down with cancer next week, they'd be there for me."

Keeping a Circle Alive

What enables a group to live long and prosper, to borrow a phrase from *Star Trek*'s Mr. Spock? A commitment to show up even when life tugs you in other directions; a willingness to let minor irritations roll off your collective backs; a common goal or passion that unites you; an effort to keep get-togethers fun or stimulating. And don't forget the brownies. Weaver, the founder of BLOWs, has this advice for starting and maintaining a committed friendship group.

1. Start a group with people you already know. It's important because you already have some trust built in and have some connection.
2. It's a fine balance between wanting intimacy and not expecting too much. Try not to put too much pressure on the women to fulfill your needs.
3. Accept people the way they are. People don't change.
4. Sometimes you don't need to dig into something. You don't need people to bare their souls all the time.
5. If a group has someone who is really difficult or has emotional problems, then in order to save the group you have to ask that person to move on in as loving a way as you can.

That happened in Ellen's book club when a self-absorbed woman hijacked every meeting with lengthy monologues about her personal problems. Someone took her aside and told her this wasn't the right group for her.

Here Today, Gone Tomorrow

My writers' circle hummed along for 1½ years, then fizzled out—at least for the time being. One woman moved to Dallas, another was overwhelmed by her parents' illnesses and family responsibilities. At the past two meetings, our "group" consisted of only me and one other person. We agreed to take a sabbatical since we all seemed to be scattered in other directions. Our group may have lived out its natural life span; perhaps we may resuscitate it down the line. Regardless, it offered us some much-needed camaraderie while it lasted. Looking back, I think our numbers were too small. While our foursome (after one woman moved) permitted intimate conversation, it also made us vulnerable to attrition. A larger gang might have maintained its momentum. But, like friendship, all groups have their own seasons.

Another friend and I just launched a short story discussion group, something we've wanted to do for years. We read short fiction by women—easier than a novel when you're busy. Since the first meeting, attendance has been fitful as women with school-age children bail out for band concerts and plays. Understandably so. Those are important. But it underscores the challenge in solidifying a new group. I'd hoped people who couldn't make one meeting would call to find out the date of the next one. But it didn't always happen.

I realize there has to be one gentle noodge who keeps kneading people together. A shepherd comes to mind. In my writers' group, I did that for a while, calling to remind people of upcoming meetings. "You're just like the dentist," one woman jibed good-naturedly, comparing me to the "You have a teeth-cleaning appointment Wednesday" phone calls. I think that's what it takes, though, in the beginning. You also need to push past any discouragement when a group doesn't immediately ignite like wildfire. You need to blow on the embers.

SAYING GOOD-BYE

And sometimes, it's simply time to go. I joined some groups that were satisfying for a while and then weren't anymore. So I left. It scared me to say good-bye, but I knew it was the right move when I didn't miss them. In fact, I felt relieved. Some gangs no longer fit. But there's always a new one. Community, in its varied shapes, is all around you, waiting for another member.

14

Sage Life-Guides

Friendships between Older and Younger Women

JENNIFER sure wasn't expecting the likes of Patricia as she clutched a bag of Meals on Wheels dinners and pressed the doorbell of the New York City apartment. Patricia, a 90-year-old former fashion designer, answered the door decked out in a silk couture blouse and black cigarette pants, her silver hair swept up in a braided bun. She invited Jennifer in for a ginger ale.

Although Jennifer didn't have time that night, she stopped in a week later, anticipating a short, polite visit. She miscalculated. The two women gabbed for three hours in Patricia's elegant apartment and munched Cheez Doodles, Patricia's favorite, until their fingers were stained orange. It was the beginning of a delicious conversation that would stretch into five years.

Jennifer, then 27, visited the widowed Patricia three nights a week and sometimes on weekends. "We used to sit there and watch the curtains blow and talk about life, art, fashion, philosophy, and love. It was like an extra grandparent, an extra best friend," says Jennifer, now 33, a university public relations manager in California. Her voice catches with emotion as she recalls her pal, who died in 1999. "Her energy and zest for life were contagious. She was everything I wanted to be when I grew up."

Patricia was fiercely independent, had traveled the world, and saw life as an adventure that was hers for the grabbing. In her friend, Jennifer saw a sharpening vision of the woman she wanted to become, like binoculars focusing on a distant image. That woman in the scope didn't need anyone's approval but her own.

"She said, 'Don't look to anybody else, look within, you know the answers,'" Jennifer recalls. "If I have a moment in my life when I need strength, I put my left hand on my right shoulder. Patricia used to come up behind me and rest her hand on my shoulder. I can feel the press of her hand and that gives me strength."

Unless you have a significantly older or younger friend, this may seem like an odd pairing. A lot of people don't have friends that span generations. Many wouldn't consider it. When your Great-Aunt Tillie is seated next to you at a wedding, you may immediately plot the earliest possible escape. How could a 35-year-old woman have much in common with a 75-year-old? But that attitude cuts you off from a fertile source of friendship.

Older women can potentially be great friends for younger women and vice versa. Someone who was fascinating and funny at 40 doesn't change because she's a few decades older. And she is more available than younger peers because she's likely retired (or working less) and her kids are grown.

Women who recognize the rich possibilities in such relationships are passionate about the rewards. Usually the age span in these duos is less dramatic than Jennifer and Patricia's 60-plus years. But they all share similar traits. A deeper layer of affection swirls beneath the friendship. They half-jokingly call each other "my surrogate mother" or "my adopted daughter" or "my extra grandmother." It's a bond, though, without the baggage that often accompanies real family. It's affection without a guilt tax.

Many women think of their elder chums as life-guides. "They're like advance scouts for me, sending dispatches back down the trail," says Ann, a 44-year-old assistant college professor with two pals in their seventies. These pairs share an alchemy that is one part age difference and one part ageless chemistry. When they are together, the years between them are at once boldly outlined and invisible.

Been There, Done That

A peer can't tell you how your life will look in ten or twenty years. She's in the same storm as you. An older friend remembers whether the sandbags worked or if you just have to watch the creek rise. She also knows the waters eventually recede. She can tell you how she survived and even thrived. The women who attract us sport scars and still-easy smiles. Soldiers. You, too, they tell us, will drink champagne and laugh when you're 75 and beyond.

These friends have already mastered the roles we're scrambling to learn. That's why Ann, the assistant college professor, turned to Ruth, 74, when she was worried about her teenage son's irrepressible high jinks at school. Just recently, he stormed the girls' dorm at his prep school with water balloons and got himself suspended. Ann anguished over whether he'd ever mature and whether her strict disciplinary response was the right one.

Over coffee at Starbucks, Ruth reassuredly patted Ann's knee and rehashed her own daughter's stormy high school years. "I had come through almost any situation a mother had ever faced. I told her how I negotiated those hairy times in our family when we were knuckle to knuckle. My daughter grew up and went to college and became the kind of kid who said, 'I love you' and

'I'm so glad you didn't let me get away with A, B, or C because deep down I didn't want to get away with it. I can see how lucky I was to have a mother who stood firm.'" Ruth promised Ann, "One day he will say, 'Thanks, Mom.' Once he finds his niche, he will blossom. This is a finite time—you'll see."

Ann often bares her frustrations to Ruth, a fiction writer, and her other older pal, Irene. "It's a reality check," she explains. "My older friends are farther down the path than I am. My view is a fixed point in space; it's that other point that helps me consider how this will be for the long run."

Kindred Spirits

Most of these spring-fall pals hook up for the same reason anyone does—they really like each other. Amy, 53, and Caitlin, 28, are certain that no matter what their ages, they would have become friends. In a theater class, where they were both earning their Ph.D.s, Caitlin admired Amy's funky retro saddle shoes. Amy complimented Caitlin's streamlined black leather bag from London. Lightning struck. "I have met very few people who talk as fast as I do and who are willing to go with a goofy idea," says Amy. "We are accomplices. We encourage in each other the qualities that a sane world might discourage." When Caitlin splurges on three pairs of shoes in a single shopping trip, Amy applauds. In turn, Amy says, "I'm writing a naughty musical and Caitlin thinks that's wonderful. She doesn't think I'm wasting my time, which I'm sure I am."

They prod each other to take risks. "She sees more possibilities," says Amy. "There are things that might stop me as an older person that wouldn't stop Caitlin and things that would stop Caitlin and I can say, 'Oh no, don't worry about that.'"

When the two women considered producing the play

Camille, the more conservative Amy worried, "We don't have the resources to do this!" "No, Amy," Caitlin corrected her. "We don't have the resources to do this *well*. I think we should borrow costumes from a friend of yours and we won't pay the actors." As Amy recalls, "We assured each other it was entirely possible. Another person might have said, 'What are you, nuts?'" They successfully produced the play in Chicago, by the way.

Amy's life experience buttressed Caitlin through the unnerving transition of taking her first real job as a professor at a university (after being a student her whole life), moving, and buying a house. The normally easygoing Caitlin was distressed that she felt so unsettled. "I said, 'You shouldn't be upset about being upset. You should be upset.' She didn't understand this would be traumatic to her," Amy says.

The fiscally minded Amy also prodded Caitlin to buy a house for the investment. "She's been encouraging me to buy a house since I was 25," laughs Caitlin. When she was teetering between a small ranch and a pricier three-bedroom split-level, Amy pointed her toward the larger home because it would be easier to resell. She also told her to buy life insurance. Her advice doesn't grate the way a mother's might. "We don't have any of the past struggles for independence. We didn't have to go through any of that thing that happens between adolescent girls and their mothers about establishing boundaries and growing up and separating. There is none of that backlog," notes Caitlin.

Mostly, though, their ages are irrelevant, a fact that is comforting to both of them. For Amy, it affirms, "I am who I am, no matter how old I am. My personality is there, Caitlin sees it, and I see hers. It's very reassuring to think, 'My gosh, I still am the person I was when I was 16.' She realizes she's the person she's going to be when she's 55." The difference in years distills the essence of their affection. "It's because our personalities sync," says Amy, not because they are neighbors or their kids play together. "We just plain enjoy each other."

KEEPER OF THE MAPS

Aging terrifies many women. But when we see others manage it gracefully and even joyfully, it instills faith in us that we can, too. Yes, advancing years will deal us some unavoidable blows. But they don't have to drag us under. Our older friends have shown us that.

Brenda studies her senior companions the way she might track a spiny path on the map of a Salt Lake City canyon where she hikes. "I'm a person who likes maps," says the 41-year-old grammar school band director. "That may be why I like older women, because they've been there." Her older friends are cartographers of her future.

"There are certain women I would like to copy when I get older and others I see as a warning sign," she says. The latter are the ones who constantly complain. Her models are women who face inexorable changes in their lives with a gentle acceptance. One older friend has failing eyesight and was dependent on her husband to read her the newspaper. She recently had to put him in a nursing home. Brenda doesn't doubt the intense loss her friend felt, but she is awed by the woman's resilience. "She is still cheerful. She rolls with the punches. I figure she's doing it. It's doable. You don't have to fall apart. She's a good example of strength."

So is Ruth Harriet Jacobs, a 78-year-old gerontologist, teacher, and author of *Be an Outrageous Older Woman*. Her younger pals watched her rebound following brain surgery several years ago. In her hospital room right before the operation, Jacobs called a friend and made a date for four months thence. "You'll never speak again. How can you make a date?" challenged a dour nurse overhearing Jacobs's optimistic plans.

Not only did Jacobs speak again, but the day they pulled out her IV tubes, she jumped into the pool for a swim. "I resumed my life. I didn't give up." She also made any necessary post-surgery adjustments with grace. Because she could no longer carry heavy books, she wheeled them in a cart to the class-room. Her hair became patchy after it was shaved for her surgery, so she amassed a collection of wild hats. "Life is a matter of changing hats for women," she says philosophically. "You can adapt."

And for Sharon, a 48-year-old artist, that willingness to adapt is evident in Naomi, her 95-year-old pal who now lives in a long-term care facility. Each morning, Naomi still fills in her eyebrows with pencil, applies foundation, and swipes her lips with cherry red. She wouldn't be caught without earrings and a necklace. She accepts her living arrangements and her macular degeneration. "She says, 'This is where I am in life,'" says Sharon. "That's what I hope I'm like when I'm that old."

A More Mellow Bond

A native Californian, Pam moved to Palm Springs from Oregon because she felt tugged home by the desert. Jewel-toned hummingbirds wove nests the size of half a walnut shell in her trees. Roadrunners sprinted across her backyard.

But there was another unexpected gift of settling in the arid town. In Oregon, she had struggled to find companions. But in Palm Springs, largely a retirement community, she found a wealth of new friends with lots of time to hike the canyons car-peted with purple wildflowers or just hang out on the porch. "Older people are better at friendship," asserts Pam, a 47-year-old nonfiction writer, who had just gone hiking the day before with a 70-year-old pal. "They have time, and time is essential." She also feels less pressure with them.

She finds that older friends focus on today in the relationship and not much beyond. "It does away with this concern, 'What's going to happen? Are we going to have a falling out? How do we maintain this friendship?' With older people, it's, 'Let's just enjoy each other.' There are not a lot of expectations about what somebody has to do to be your friend."

NO-COMPETITION CLAUSE

Pam and other women describe another benefit of older companions: relief from the competition and jealousy that often pock even the best friendships with contemporaries. "I have friends going back to third grade. When we get together there is still this way we are comparing. Who's doing better? Who's doing more? It's the way you measure your own progress. It's a legitimate evolutionary thing. Do I have enough nuts stored for the winter?" says Pam.

Older friends don't compare careers or country homes. "There's a mellowness that comes with being toward the end of your life. You don't have to impress each other," Pam says.

Indeed, the absence of jealousy made it easier for Ann, the assistant college professor, to consult her "council of elders" rather than her contemporaries when she was debating whether to accept an assistant professor's post. She feared asking the opinion of a friend who was a colleague, concerned the job offer could spark resentment. "She'd think, if it was a good job, 'Why didn't they contact me?' and if it wasn't, she'd denigrate it," Ann predicted. Instead, Ann's two "surrogate mothers" helped her weigh the offer. Irene drove her to the school to check out the commute. "Too far!" she said. Ruth shared stories of her own teaching days. She helped Ann realize that what sounded like a modest commitment could swallow much more of her time than she expected. With their guidance, Ann turned it down. A better offer turned up a few months later.

BEYOND MENTORING

Some relationships take seed as mentor and protégée, then evolve to deeper strata. Laura struck up a conversation with Sonia, a well-known author she recognized, while they were sitting on a bench during the intermission of a play about Kafka. During a brief but intense chat, Laura confessed she wanted to write "but didn't have the chutzpah to go after it." Sonia advised Laura to "go where the fear is."

Laura felt so drawn to Sonia, she tracked down her e-mail address at San Diego State University where she taught and sent her a note saying how much the advice meant to her. Thus began daily missives about their personal lives and Sonia's efforts to help Laura achieve her longtime dream of writing greeting cards. "She's taught me to forget the 'someday' and go after it now," Laura, 40, says. But the relationship soon morphed beyond career support. "She gives me a lot of advice—get outside, take vitamin D, take your calcium. She checks to see if I got my mammogram."

"I love her like my own kids. She's my cyberkid," says Sonia, who is 74.

Laura has always been drawn to older women because she has more in common with them. "I can have conversations with more depth with older people than I can have with my peers. I am not someone who gravitates to conversations about who I met at the bar or what I should wear. When I was a teenager and my friends were trying on their Jordache jeans, I was talking with their parents."

What's in It for Me?

It may seem like these friendships are a one-way street—the older woman giving and the younger one taking. But there are plenty of perks on both sides of the equation. Meeting a younger friend is like throwing open a window on a warm, breezy day. As Ruth, the fiction writer, says, "I have a lot of friends who are dealing with health problems. Seeing someone like Ann who is so sunny and, thank heavens, healthy, is like spring coming after winter. Many of my friends are in the winter or fall of their lives. Being connected to Ann brings an extra measure of optimism. I have a lovely friendship with a woman who has so many years ahead of her. It makes me feel like I have all those years ahead of me, though I know damn well I don't. I keep thinking the best is yet to come. She's young and maybe it makes me feel that I'm young."

Author Barbara Quick relishes the tornado of energy that is her 15-years-junior friend, Jennifer—the same Jennifer who was Patricia's friend in New York City. "She has a wonderful, fresh perspective on life. She is full of excitement," says Quick, who penned *Under Her Wing: The Mentors Who Changed Our Lives*. Quick, who lives in northern California, also enjoys Jennifer's unvarnished admiration. "Jennifer really appreciates me in a way that helps me appreciate myself. She's very supportive of who I am."

Younger friends are also insurance for the future, which is something Jacobs discovered through her students, who have since become close pals. Jacobs's life teems with younger buddies—swimming companions she sees at 5:30 every morning at the health club pool and former students who often visit her at home. When she had the brain surgery, one former student drove her to the hospital for tests, one grocery shopped, another cooked lasagna dinners. "It eased the burden on my son and daughter," Jacobs says, as well as her contemporaries, a lot of whom ship off to winter homes in Florida or Hawaii. "They're still your friends, but they're not around for you," she notes.

Others have become ill with Alzheimer's or died of cancer. "If all your friends are your age or older, you may eventually find yourself without friends," she warns.

Her junior buddies also illuminate the lives of her adult children. "Your friends can straighten you out as to how to act appropriately with your daughters and sons," says Jacobs, a visiting scholar at the Center for Research on Women at Wellesley College. "I can understand my daughter's work life better and not be so demanding of her time because I see how busy the midlife women are who are my friends. So I don't think my daughter's neglecting me if she doesn't have time to do things." Conversely, an older pal can offer insight into a younger woman's mother. "It can make her more understanding of her own mother's needs and frailties," adds Jacobs.

As Jacobs discovered, younger women can be surrogate daughters for their older friends, especially those whose own children are flung across the country. But even if they assume a daughterly role, it's a freer one than with their real moms because they don't feel as judged or worried about. Therefore, it's often easier for a woman to confide in an older friend instead of her mother. "I would never hesitate to tell Patricia anything," says Jennifer, "but I would hesitate to tell my mother. Patricia would never worry. She knew I could take care of myself."

A Shorter Season and Other Considerations

Women know they have abbreviated time with their older friends. "I'm always aware that I won't have Ruth as a friend forever. For other people I would never think that," observes Ann. "I know the day will come when I will have to go to her funeral."

These bonds may also present some extra challenges. A significantly older pal may have physical limitations—she likely

How to Pick Up Older Women

Older women are all around you—in your church or synagogue, in classes, in clubs. You also could troll for an older friend at a senior center in your community. Ask the activities director how to get involved or to recommend someone for you to meet. Perhaps you could break the ice by interviewing her on tape about her life. Another possibility for pals is in elderly housing. A resident service coordinator in one of these buildings may be able to direct you to someone or invite you to meet people in an activity or community room. And memoir writing classes tend to attract women who are looking back on long, full lives.

won't be the one you'll invite for a long bike ride. (On the other hand, we all know some pretty athletic older people who might be thinking the same thing about us!) There may be financial differences between generations, as well. A friend with a few more decades under her belt may have less money if she's living off retirement savings. Or if she grew up during the Depression, she may cinch her purse strings tight. When Jacobs went to a Turkish restaurant with an 86-year-old friend, the woman took one look at the $9 sandwiches and $14 salads and insisted they leave for cheaper climes—even though Jacobs offered to treat. They had to trudge several blocks to a less costly spot.

What Goes Around Comes Around

In the recesses of younger women's minds is the hope that when they advance to the elder generation, they will find younger friends like themselves. "What goes around comes around," says a 47-year-old woman who takes her 97-year-old neighbor out to lunch, not minding the slow-paced walk from the car to the restaurant. "There's a part of me that hopes if I live that long, there will be someone that will want to be with me, too."

15

Just Your Type

⊶

The Burgeoning World of Internet Pals

BRIDGETTE was 37, three months pregnant, and didn't know another soul who was having a baby. Most of her friends were either single or putting their kids through college. There was nobody she could ask why the short walk from the car to her university classes left her breathless or why the smell of macaroni and cheese made her feel dangerously queasy. And she knew her circle of friends wasn't interested in updates on every movement of the baby, as much as those stirrings thrilled her.

But then Bridgette, a computer specialist from Orange County, California, discovered a pregnancy e-mail list organized by the months women were due to give birth. With the click of a mouse she was instantly connected to more than 100 women with whom she happily swapped the details of each other's pregnancies. "She moved!" typed Bridgette. "How did it feel?" dozens of women asked. "Like butterflies!" she zipped back. She also shared every icy jab of fear, such as when the doctor thought he had found an extra chromosome in an early prenatal test. While she waited the two terrifying weeks for the results of her amniocentesis, e-mail friends showered her with daily messages of support. "It was like having sisters waiting with me for the test results," recalls Bridgette, who learned that the "extra chromosome" was merely a speck on the film.

"They understood me and supported me more than some of my face-to-face friends. They were my safety net," says Bridgette. It was a diverse "net," consisting of college professors, a NASA scientist, a writer for ABC news, a former professional ice skater, and at-home moms.

Then, on her 40th birthday, an unsuspecting Bridgette walked into a San Francisco restaurant. "Surprise!" shouted forty of her e-mail-list friends, who had flown in from as far away as Arizona and Canada to celebrate. "Oh, my God, I can't believe people did this for me," the stunned, tearful birthday girl kept repeating. She and her pals spent the weekend sightseeing. She drove home in a car overflowing with gifts.

A Fertile Field

Not everyone who has made friends online gets thrown a surprise birthday weekend, but the rest of Bridgette's story is not unusual. Women have been amassing friends on the Internet since e-mail exploded over the past decade. Some nab pals there more easily than in their own backyards, meeting on diverse Web sites for book discussion groups, guinea pig owners, scrapbooking enthusiasts, feminist moms, and career networking. Cyberspace pals have become a lifeline for those who stay home with children, have felt isolated after a move, work at home, have a disability, or are simply shy.

Although sociologists warned of the Internet's potential to yank us away from our local communities and accelerate our social isolation, in many cases the opposite seems true. In a rising trend, more people are meeting online friends in person. A 2001 UCLA Internet Report by the university's Center for Communication Policy found that almost 19 percent of Internet users had gone on to meet their online friends. The study found that they had met six people from online contacts, an increase over the previous year's 12 percent of Internet users meeting five online acquaintances.

Women in list groups are flying across the country and sometimes the world to greet each other at conventions. Neighbors connect on Internet groups and begin going out for coffee. The Web has also helped women rediscover long-lost pals. While a few perils do tag along with the perks—e-mail lists can be time vacuums and ripe ground for spreading gossip—clearly, the old notion of community has been flipped upside down. E-mail friends send shower gifts or show up at a virtual pal's door to help out when her husband is critically ill. There's nothing isolating about that.

CYBERFRIENDSHIPS BLOSSOM FASTER

Friendships seem to take root and flourish more quickly in cyberspace, as if they were being sprinkled with Miracle Gro. That's partly because some women seem more comfortable revealing themselves on the computer screen. Reflecting alone in front of a blank screen inspires self-revelation in the way of a diary or journal. It's safer and easier to unsheathe your deeper self to someone whom you won't bump into squeezing the cantaloupes at the grocery store. The very nature of writing slices through the airy social chitchat that frustrates many women. There are no dissatisfying "Hihowareyou? Finehowareyou?"

exchanges. "You have a tendency to talk about more intimate things online," says one woman. "Your close circle of friends in real life often has a vested interest in some of what you're doing and saying. If I've been a friend to your husband for 10 years, you may not be so willing to say something negative about him." The confessionals to relative strangers that would seem inappropriate in a new face-to-face relationship don't raise an eyebrow in cyberspace.

Many women crave daily contact with friends but would feel like pests if they phoned once a day. But that reluctance evaporates with electronic missives, a communication that never intrudes or interrupts anybody while she's eating dinner. And in cyberspace there is no telephone tag, no forgotten phone calls. There's a satisfying immediacy to messages that drop a friend into the thick of your experience, whether it's swooning over a new flavor of Ben & Jerry's or steaming over a boss's critical comment. And you don't have to synchronize schedules to "talk." You can write to your friend at midnight when you can't sleep; she can respond at 10 A.M.

A BRIDGE FOR SHY WOMEN

For women who are shy or insecure, e-mail friendships fling open previously locked doors. "I struggle all the time with not quite fitting in," admits Bridgette, who says her self-consciousness inhibits her from making friends. "I feel like I never have the right makeup and the right clothes. In e-mail you can be a human being without the garbage of having somebody judge you for what you wear. E-mail friends see what's inside you first." And the Internet cracked open a vast new world of hearing friends for Katrina, who is deaf. "I'm able to do so many things online that strip away the communication barriers," writes Katrina, 34, a Chicago-area family support specialist for the parents of deaf children.

It's also a preferred social arena for loners like Donna, 42, an Internet business owner in Houston. All of her friends, including her best friend in Georgia, are online. She's never met any of them. "For me, cyberfriendships are perfect. When I feel like socializing, I socialize. When I don't, I don't have to answer my e-mail. I can better manage my time without girlfriends dropping by. I don't have to block out half a day to see a friend. I can pick and choose when I want to converse. I don't have to talk to anyone all day if I don't want to."

Making It Real

But e-mail is still a narrow aperture setting on a relationship. You can't hug a cyberspace friend or see her smile. Many women want to meet their Internet pals to make them real.

When my New York online friend, Sally, announced she was coming to Chicago for a business trip last spring, I was torn. A story deadline was breathing down my neck, but it would be fun to meet. I pushed work aside and hopped a train downtown. Boy, was it worth it. Sitting across the breakfast table from Sally that spring morning, seeing the crinkle of her eyes when she laughed (which she did often), hearing her endearing New York vowels, and feeling the warmth she radiated, painted her in vivid hues. It linked us in a way electronics could not. When I e-mail her now, I see her and hear her voice. Because in-person conversations spontaneously swerve into unplanned territory, we discovered things about each other that day that we likely never would have learned in our 20-line missives. One was that we both have disabled brothers. She finagled a business trip to my town so we can get together again. I can't wait to see her.

These "first dates" are happening all over the country. When Bridgette, the Orange County woman, discovered one of her e-mail pals lived only 80 miles away, the two began visiting once

a month. And Bridgette's virtual chum from Norway flew over
and spent a week with her. Susan, an at-home mom from Jack-
sonville, Florida, discovered a woman on her feminist moms
e-mail list was actually a neighbor. They now have coffee on
Friday nights. "The list has enlarged my support network in real
life," Susan says.

Internet friends are also packing their bags to meet at conventions. Stephanie, 40, a church communications director in
Dallas, flew to Orlando to vacation with all the parents who had
been communicating on a Web site for kids with diabetes.
"Meeting all those women was a teary-eyed moment. It's not
like meeting someone for the first time. It's more like meeting a
soul mate, because you know her ins and outs, and your friendship has already evolved through e-mail," Stephanie says. But
now she could wipe away a tear and give them an "atta-girl"
high five. She hung out at the pool with the five women she had
been e-mailing individually for more than a year. "It was like a
sorority," she says. "It reminded me of a little girl's birthday party
where she's got her best friends and they are sitting around in a
circle giggling."

Just a few years ago Stephanie's close friendships were all
online. But now she wants the electricity that crackles through
a live group. "I want a conversational frenzy. When five moms
are talking at one time you can't wait to chime in, you can't
wait to participate. You can't have a frenzy with e-mail. A chat
room isn't the same. You need the personal face-to-face, touch-
to-touch. It cannot be beat," she stresses. To snare friends in her
town, she created a local e-mail list of parents with diabetic
children. She invites them to margarita parties at her house
and organizes family roller-skating and water park outings. "I
realized while standing in a grocery line, this person could be
on my list and I wouldn't know them from Adam. I don't think

online relationships are enough for a deeper commitment in a friendship."

NERVOUS FIRST MEETINGS

For some women, the excitement of that initial in-person meeting tangles with anxiety. "I was very anxious that once they saw what I looked like they wouldn't want to know me anymore," says one woman before her first "reunion" of her e-mail-list friends. "I think several other moms were worried about that, too. Some tried to lose weight!"

"Maybe it's insecurity," suggests another woman. "Am I going to be the person she thinks I am from my e-mail? But once you put a voice and face to the words you've been reading, those little barriers come tumbling down."

Still, the social realities of physically being in a room with thirty women, rather than talking via e-mail posts, mean some cliques form and some feelings may be hurt. That's what happened in one woman's gathering of list members from around the country. The women had all been on level ground when they were chatting online, but that changed when they met in person. The women with more expensive clothes and an education split from some of the others and went to a nicer restaurant for dinner. After the meeting, some women were so upset about the cliquishness, they left the list.

Amazing Acts of Friendship

E-mail friendships inspire support that leaps off the screen into stunning generosity in real life. When a woman on a list was unable to afford a bike for her son's birthday, several members pitched in and mailed her the money to buy one. After torrential rains flooded another woman's house in North Carolina, e-mail friends shipped her kids clothes and called the local Home Depot, which donated materials to help her rebuild. An e-mail pal of a Chicago woman, whose husband had been hospitalized for months with cancer, flew in for a week to help cook meals for her family and watch her kids. The woman was from an Internet group of mothers who had adopted children from Russia. They collected money and sent the Chicago woman $400 worth of groceries and dinner for Mother's Day.

In another compassionate act, the cyberfriends of a young woman who has terminal cancer are holding fundraisers and establishing a foundation to benefit her kids. Because the women are part of a scrapbooking group, they are also crafting an album with her children's photos with space for her to write her thoughts and create a legacy for them. A woman couldn't ask for more from her face-to-face friends.

Tripping on E-Mail Land Mines

But Internet friendships, like any face-to-face friendships, have downsides. They can suck up gobs of time for women trying to keep up with multiple lists. And women hiding behind the anonymity of their computers are more brazen about dissing people on their list—called flaming. There is also a greater potential for misunderstanding a missive than a real conversation.

WHAT DID YOU MEAN BY THAT?

The written word, devoid of subtle voice shadings and facial expressions, is susceptible to misinterpretation. That can cause confusion and missteps between electronic friends. One of my friend's e-mail messages sounded angry and caustic for no reason I could fathom. I was dumbstruck. Then I wrote back asking about it. She had been kidding, but without seeing her wry smile or hearing the playfulness in her voice, I couldn't tell. "Sometimes things come across harsher than you meant them. They sound more stark," says Diana, 34, who has dozens of on-line friends. "If you put LOL [laughing out loud] behind it, everyone knows it's a joke."

But the opportunity to edit your words usually smoothes communication. Notes Diana: "I have a chance to order my thoughts and make them sound the best that I can. When it comes out of my mouth, sometimes things slip out before I have a chance to stop myself. I'll say something stupid. I can't hit delete. That's what's good about the computer: you can take it back if you're careful before you send it." And the very act of ex-pressing disgruntled feelings on a screen is sometimes enough in itself, she points out. "You've gotten it out and it's over. Once it's on paper, it doesn't seem as serious or as important, or maybe that's not really how you feel." The message doesn't al-ways need to be sent.

GOSSIP FLIES FAR AND FAST

Stephanie, in Dallas, has already tripped over a hazard of e-mail lists. The cloak of the screen and the ease of zipping mes-sages to large groups creates a potential breeding ground for gossipmongering. A woman whom Stephanie suspects is jealous of her electronically slammed her to everyone on their list. That's the equivalent of 100 nasty phone calls. "People have more guts to do this because of the safety behind the screen. They can do some serious damage if they have a demented mind-set, which this person does," she says. Stephanie zinged an angry message back to the offender, who had backstabbed her online before. "My tolerance for your antics has finally ex-pired," she wrote, forwarding her message to the entire list. "I said if she has a problem with what I say, address it with me directly." In the e-mail, Stephanie invited members (a local group) to a party at her house. "Your family," she informed the woman, "will not be included." The woman has not posted on the list since.

Flame wars also can erupt on e-mail lists. That's when members' disagreements devolve into sniping personal attacks. A well-operated list should have a moderator to screen rude behavior. Repeat offenders may be removed from a list. Some lists even have "netiquette" rules on proper communications to guide you.

SO MANY E-MAILS, NOT ENOUGH TIME

The cybercommunity can become a time vacuum, sucking up critical hours from a woman's marriage, family, and work. "I spend too much time chatting and not enough time 'living' with my children," confesses Diana, an at-home New Jersey mom with four children ages 8, 7, 3, and 1. Diana, who is active on 10 e-mail lists, receives about 150 e-mails a day that she feels obligated to read. She spends an hour in the morning responding to messages, pops online throughout the day for 15-minute intervals, and spends 2 more hours at night.

For her the cybercommunity is a powerful, sometimes irresistible lure. "Addiction is not a bad word for it," she admits. One recent morning she needed to get her kids dressed to go outside and play but had trouble tearing herself away from her mail. "I'll say, 'One more minute.' They say, 'You're always on AOL! You're always getting your mail!' It's a constant evaluation of what your priorities are. I'll hear a little voice saying, 'What's more important? You really have to give your kids lunch.' The littler ones get pretty cranky with me."

One night her husband, whose own computer sits next to hers, was trying to snag her attention to check out a cybertour of a car he planned to buy. In the midst of reading e-mails about a new crafts store that had opened in her neighborhood, Diana reluctantly turned to his screen, issued a perfunctory "Beautiful!" and spun back to her cyberchat. "I felt a little guilty," she says.

Perhaps the Internet's draw is a measure of how much she and other women yearn to be with friends and tied to a community. Indeed, in the three years after Diana graduated from college and moved back to New Jersey to marry and work, she didn't have a single close friend. When she decided to stay home with her first child, "I was the only stay-at-home mom on my road. They were the loneliest years of my life," she says. "I had acquaintances, but not a single woman I could count on to call if I needed help."

Not anymore. Many of Diana's e-mail friends are from lists of New Jersey women who are passionate about scrapbooking. After meeting online, they see each other at weekend workshops or conventions. "I have a very satisfying friendship with these women over the Internet. I probably wouldn't have met them if it hadn't been for the computer," says Diana. "There would have been little opportunity for our paths to cross except in an online community. I don't know what my life would be like if I didn't have these friendships." Her e-mail connections extend beyond her immediate town. "If I want to visit my family in North Carolina, I know five or six other women I can visit, too." She tracks the lives of her close online friends, knowing one was just in a car accident, one just had a baby, and another is being hospitalized with postpartum depression.

The challenge for Diana is balancing her electronic life with her flesh-and-blood existence. "I'm working harder on confining my e-mail stuff. E-mail is clutter in my life. It grows and grows. I'm trying to organize it and stuff it back in the closet."

Rekindling Old Friendships

Maintaining a long-distance friendship is like trying to hold water in your hands. After my friend Caroline relocated from Dallas, where we'd both lived, to Washington, D.C., I resettled in Chicago. We promised to keep in touch. Who doesn't? But our phone calls trailed farther apart. Our chats, once spontaneous and heartfelt, turned into "news updates," an unsatisfying reporting of big events like you might do with a distant cousin at a family reunion. We had slipped from each other's lives because we lost the details. It made me sad.

Then we got e-mail. Our friendship recharged with a vengeance as we reclaimed the minutiae of each other's days. "Steve was in a huff because the kids said they like my scrambled eggs better than his. Mine are soft and creamy because I cook them on low. His are hard because he cooks them on high," she e-mailed me one morning. I felt like I was in her kitchen.

I ranted to her about my dorky new haircut minutes after I got home and looked in the mirror. She knew when I was annoyed at my husband as soon as the door slammed when he left for work. It was almost as good as being able to stop by her desk in our former office.

Lara, a computer systems analyst from Chicago, hasn't lived in the same state as her old college pal, Monica, since 1979. Their once tight relationship had also waned, but e-mail resuscitated them. Now Lara knows Monica is cooking salmon ravioli for dinner and whether she has fulfilled her dream of being named volunteer of the week at her children's school. "It's been almost 300 weeks of failure," notes a sympathetic Lara. Monica knows that Lara is suffering from a nasty case of blisters because she can't find a good pair of walking socks. "I can imagine myself in her house, seeing the kids coming and going, seeing the spats with her husband. I really do feel almost like I'm her next-door neighbor," Lara says happily.

WHATEVER HAPPENED TO LIZ?

Another promising route to cyberfriendship is tracking down childhood pals. It's a way to pick up a live thread of a once-close relationship. The urge seems to strike women when they reach midlife, spurring millions of visits to classmate Web sites.

During their high school years, Marti spent more time at Liz's house than her own. They slipped intricately folded notes into each other's lockers three times a day—their loopy script detailing the trivia of classes and social dramas. But the girls were separated when Liz moved out of state her senior year. Then Liz went to college, while Marti married and had three kids. They dashed off occasional cards and letters for a while, but then troubled marriages, divorces, and numerous moves frayed their communications. When they tried to track each other down again, they dialed disconnected phone numbers and wrote to out-of-date addresses.

"There wasn't a day that went by that I didn't think about her and wonder where she was. I felt like I had lost my right arm," says Marti, 51, a social worker at a Boston hospital. Her father passed away on Liz's birthday, and she couldn't call her friend to tell her. Some days, to feel her friend's presence, Marti reread Liz's decade-old letters.

Then, in March 2001, Marti was scrolling through the list for her 1968 graduating class on www.classmates.com. Liz's name leaped out at her. She stared in disbelief, then quickly shelled over the membership fee so she could contact her. "Are you for real?" Marti typed hopefully. "Of course, it's me!" answered a joyful Liz the next day. In what seemed like fate, Liz had entered her name in the Classmates.com directory just two weeks earlier in the hope that her old friend would find her.

Several months later, Liz, a technical writer in Virginia, made a visit. When Marti strode into the cavernous train station waiting room, she instantly recognized her friend, who was toting an enormous suitcase stuffed with every photo album she owned. In Marti's suburban living room, the women gently held 17 years of photographs and stared at each other's children and family members whose growth they had missed. "We must have gone through 2,000 photos between the two of us," says Marti. Reflects Liz, "It was like having the other half of yourself back,

---

How to Find Online Friends

You don't need a private detective to sleuth out an old friend. Many women reconnect through reunion Web sites such as www.classmates.com or by typing a name into www.google.com for clues to her whereabouts. Also try typing "finding old friends" into a Google.com search for other Web sites that help locate pals.

To develop friends online, find groups that match your passions, hobbies, lifestyle, or work via Web sites such as Google.com or www.yahoo.com and clicking on "groups." There are also several online women's networks, such as www.women.com and www.ivillage.com, that contain chat rooms and message boards that are interest-specific. The site Bridgette used while she was pregnant, www.parenting.com, also has message boards for women with babies up to one year old. Also, try the Web site of a national organization that supports your interests. Once you're on an e-mail list, you will likely find a few people you want to communicate with individually. That's the first step in an electronic friendship.

And always use caution online. "Check for credentials and the validity of the group," advises Stephanie, who met other parents via a Web site for kids with diabetes. "You have to use common sense. You don't meet an online knitting friend in a dark alley in the middle of the night. Don't give your address or phone number out to people until you feel very comfortable with them."

somebody who knew who you were, who you didn't have to explain yourself to."

But in the midst of the happy reunion, a submerged pain resurfaced for Marti. "I had always felt like the dumb one. I almost didn't make it through high school. I was incredibly embarrassed by that. All that crap came rolling back," she says. Marti later discovered she had a learning disability and went to college in her thirties. She admitted to Liz how humiliated she had felt. But Liz had viewed her friend differently. She had seen a bright, funny girl with an uncanny ability to understand people. "They were things I never saw in myself," says a stunned Marti. "She took the pain away." On her desk, Marti prominently displays a photo of Liz dancing at Marti's son's wedding—which marked her second visit. "I felt like there was a big hole in my life for a long time," says Marti, "and now it's filled."

⚬━✦━⚬

Bridgette's computer crashed recently. The screen went blank on her 50 friendships. "I can't communicate with some of my best friends," she moaned after two weeks of a fried hard drive. These are the women who not only threw her a surprise 40th birthday party but also supported her when her 71-year-old mother died of a heart attack before her eyes. "What do you need right now?" they asked her then. Bridgette's Italian mother had been a terrific cook, and Bridgette mentioned that she craved rigatoni. It reminded her of her mom. After the funeral, three huge trays of rigatoni—compliments of her cyberfriends—were delivered to her house. When the computer is fixed—in a few more days, she prays—she'll race to read all the communiqués from her pals and write back. Then, she says, "my lifeline will have been restored."

Afterword

LONELINESS stinks, but you're not stuck there forever. If your circle of friends has atrophied or you've always come up short— that's not your destiny. It wasn't mine and it's not yours. Sure, there were times when I was so discouraged that I threw up my hands and said, "It's not worth it. It's too hard!" But a few weeks or months passed and I met somebody who was kind, made me laugh, and I thought, *maybe*. Three of those maybes turned into wonderful friends. And one hibernating pal awoke and spun back into my life, thanks to an effort by both of us.

The women who have shared their stories here have taught me a lot. They made me smarter, more generous, more for-giving. Every friendship is a book with unwritten chapters. That's part of the journey—and the challenge. If there's any-thing I've learned, it's to take the long view: I may disappoint you today, but hopefully I'll come through tomorrow. It's better to air a grievance than to pull away. And broken friendships can often be repaired.

The tango isn't always easy. But it's worth it.

Notes

Supplementary Sources

CHAPTER 2

Bowling Alone by Robert Putnam (Simon & Schuster, 2002) *
The General Social Survey from the University of Chicago's National Opinion Research Center found that women are spending less time with their neighbors.* John Cacioppo, a social neuroscientist at the University of Chicago, found that feeling isolated alters our personality. In one part of a study, he evaluated the personality traits of lonely students at Ohio State. He found they were more anxious, hostile, pessimistic, and stressed. Then, at Stanford University, Cacioppo and coresearchers hypnotized students, suggesting that they experience loneliness. During the hypnosis session, scientists evaluated the students' personalities and found they now exhibited the same traits as the chronically lonely Ohio State students. Cacioppo had originally wondered if the Ohio State kids were lonely because their personalities turned people off. He learned, instead, that feeling alienated affected their behavior.

CHAPTER 3

Time for Life: The Surprising Ways Americans Use Their Time by John P. Robinson and Geoffrey Godbey (The Pennsylvania State University Press, 1997)

CHAPTER 6

Joanne H. Pratt Associates provided the figure of 3.25 million operating home-based businesses.

CHAPTER 10

The Tending Instinct by Shelley E. Taylor (Times Books, 2002) * *Social Epidemiology* edited by Lisa F. Berkman and Ichiro Kawachi (Oxford University Press, 2000) * *Health and Ways of Living: The Alameda County Study* by Lisa F. Berkman and Lester Breslow (Oxford University Press, 1983) * "Social Support Versus Companionship: Effects on Life Stress, Loneliness, and Evaluations by Others" by Karen S. Rook, in *Journal of Personality and Social Psychology* (Vol. 52, no. 6, pp. 1132–1147, 1987) * "The Negative Side of Social Interaction: Impact on Psychological Well-Being" by Karen S. Rook, in *Journal of Personality and Social Psychology* (Vol. 46, no. 5, pp. 1097–1108, 1984) * "Gender, Social Support, and Cardiovascular Responses to Stress" by Laura M. Glynn et al., in *Psychosomatic Medicine* (Vol. 61, pp. 234–242, 1999) * "Sex-Specific Effects of Social Support on Cortisol and Subjective Responses to Acute Psychological Stress" by C. Kirschbaum et al., in *Psychosomatic Medicine* (Vol. 57, no. 1, pp. 23–31, 1995) * I am grateful to Dr. Redford Williams for explaining the impact of stress on the body.

CHAPTER 13

Creating Community Anywhere: Finding Support and Connection in a Fragmented World by Carolyn R. Shaffer and Kristin Anundsen (Jeremy P. Tarcher/Perigee Books, 1993) * "The Relational Health Indices: A Study of Women's Relationships" by Belle Liang et al., in *Psychology of Women Quarterly*

(Vol. 26, pp. 25–35, 2002) * "A Family of Friends" by Ann Japenga, in *Health* (November/December, pp. 91–97, 1995)

Recommended Reading

Best Friends: The Pleasures and Perils of Girls' and Women's Friendships by Terri Apter and Ruthellen Josselson (Crown, 1998) * *The Dance of Anger* by Harriet Lerner (HarperCollins, 2001) * *The Healing Connection: How Women Form Relationships in Therapy and in Life* by Jean Baker Miller and Irene Pierce Stiver (Beacon Press, 1998) * *Will This Place Ever Feel Like Home? Simple Advice for Settling In after Your Move* by Leslie Levine (Contemporary Books, 2002) * *Staying Home: From Full-Time Professional to Full-Time Parent* by Darcie Sanders and Martha M. Bullen (Spencer & Waters, 2001) * *Between Women: Love, Envy, and Competition in Women's Friendships* by Luise Eichenbaum and Susie Orbach (Viking, 1988).